100
SOCIAL INNOVATION
FROM FINLAND

Edited by
Ilkka Taipale

FINNISH LITERATURE SOCIETY 2013

Kirjokansi 27
2nd revised edition

Translations: Zona Sur, Don McCracken, Eva Malkki,
Pilvi Riikka Taipale and authors www.finlit.fi

ISBN 978-952-222-463-7
ISSN 2323-7392

Printed in ScandBook AB, Falun 2013

FOREWORD OF THE SECOND EDITION

Docent Ilkka Taipale has claimed that "When a coin is put on my ear or I when a beer reaches my mouth, I immediately get a useful idea". This catalogue of Finnish social innovations is one of those ideas.

Usually the word "innovation" refers to developing new material objects or commercial services, but innovations can also be social in nature: social innovations are practical solutions that promote citizens' participation, standard of living, health, education and other forms of wellbeing.

It is a good idea to broaden the concept of innovation. Wellbeing is founded not just on technical developments but also on social innovations.

The book contains different kinds of highly diverse social innovations, which make it an engaging and interesting read. Innovations cannot be classed in any rational way according to how good, important and inventive they are. There are practical solutions and things that make everyday life that little bit easier, as well as hugely important political decisions and social politics that have had a beneficial effect on the nation's wellbeing.

My own favourite innovation concerns the creation of more opportunities for equality. Free education and student grants have made education available to everyone, regardless of their social or economic background.

The book also includes innovations whose developers have a good sense of humour. An interesting example of this is the highly popular traditional board game African Star.

According to former chief editor Aimo Kairamo, "It is always worth giving Taipale money for whatever reason he needs it because it always goes to a worthy cause." This book that Docent Ilkka Taipale has edited is a good example of that. It has already been translated into many languages – Finland's social innovations are also interesting to people outwith our national borders. Promoting and ensuring wellbeing requires ongoing development and renewal. I hope that this book encourages pioneers in different fields to create new and even better innovations than before.

Sauli Niinistö
President of the Republic of Finland

FOREWORD OF THE FIRST EDITION

The world is changing rapidly, so how can we surmount the challenges of the future? We must be able to broaden our perspective. In Finland, as in many other countries, methods and systems have been created to promote innovations and capitalise on them. Success is not founded on science or technical inventions alone, however, although they are a great help.

Finland's strong competitivity and high standard of living are based on the Nordic welfare society, which motivates individual effort and self-development, but also provides communal support. Democracy, respect for human rights and the principle of a constitutional state, as well as good governance, are a solid base for a society. In Finland the State and the municipalities play essential roles in social welfare and health, as well as education and research, but citizens themselves also keep the system alive through their role as initiators and service providers in different non-governmental organisations.

All five Nordic countries enjoy great success in international comparisons on e.g. competitivity, sustainable development and lack of corruption. The hundred-odd articles in this book describe a diverse and interesting array of social innovations. They provide an insight into Finnish society and the way it works, and I believe that the reader can also find feasible ideas that could be applied elsewhere. Many of the social innovations are universal to some extent, but there are also some engaging differences.

Many of the innovations introduced in this book have been successfully implemented in Finland over the decades, and this will probably continue into the foreseeable future.

The globalising world might involve new challenges that must be taken into account, however, and their resolution might require new innovations. Our future aim is to combine the welfare society with competitivity. They are not enemies, but partners.

Doctor Ilkka Taipale, the editor and author of three of the articles in this book, can with good reason be considered a social innovator. He still participates actively in public debate, lobbying for Finnish social policies and innovations that can improve the position of the most vulnerable people in our society.

I believe that this book will give rise to new ideas and encourage you to see the world with new eyes.

Tarja Halonen
President of Finland, 2000–2012

INTRODUCTION

When Mohandas Ghandi was asked, "what do you think about Western civilization?" he replied, "I think it would be a good idea."

The Nordic welfare model has been marketed by exaggerating its positive aspects: Nordic countries are successful states. The Finnish Ministry of Foreign Affairs published a booklet at the beginning of the century about the success of the Nordic countries in relation to other places which included a lot of hype, but happily at the end of the book there were a couple of pages in a Memento mori (remember that you are dying) chapter which reminded us of "Nordic stumbling blocks" in the form of poverty and those who have fallen through the safety net, along with other unsolved social problems.

For too long we have been blind to anything other than technical innovations and based the economy on these alone. The Technical Research Centre of Finland (VTT), the Finnish Funding Agency for Technology and Innovation (Tekes), The Finnish Innovation Fund SITRA, technical universities, Nokia, Kone and other technology companies are at the cutting edge, and almost 4 percent of Finland's Gross National Product is devoted to research and development.

However, the beginning of the 1990s saw more discussion about social innovations too – innovations that could not be patented – many of which are the corner stones of the welfare state: our parliamentary democracy, equality between men and women, municipal independence, universal social security that excludes no one, free education and comprehensive literacy, and the peaceful society that has been created by these elements.

This book is comprised of 100 social innovations from Finland, and the writers are a wonderful group who have developed or adapted them. They are of different ages with different ideologies and they come from different parts of society, but they all represent both the serious and entertaining nature of the innovations. The book includes such diverse ideas as the single-chamber parliament and dish-drying cupboard, child day care and public laundering jetties, working bees and tripartism and coalition government, Linux and Father Christmas. Even with all that has been included, however, there has not been room for everything and a number of worthwhile social innovations have had to be omitted.

It is an interesting phenomenon that the first publication of this book in 2006 – during Finland's second term holding the presidency of the EU – failed to attract much interest in the country. The matters presented in this book are taken completely for granted in much the same way as clean drinking water, as in Finland water can be consumed from any tap in the country and in fact directly from any of 100,000 lakes without fear of becoming sick. However, when thousands became ill in the town of Nokia (from where the phone company takes its name) when the clean water and waste water pipes were accidentally switched, it made people aware that things that they take for granted should be valued more highly.

Now that the book has been made available abroad (it has currently been published in fifteen languages – Arabia, English, Finnish, Japanese, Korean, Latvian, Lithuanian, Mandarin Chinese, Mongolia, Portuguese, Polish, Punjabi, Russian, Spanish, Swedish, Ukrainian and Urdu, and it will be translated into at least Arabic, Bengali, Farsi, Hindi, Mongolian and Pashtun), however, it has made Finns sit up and take notice of the things they have forgotten to notice.

I am happy so see that this year will also see the publication of another book: "100 technical and scientific innovations from Finland". One of my favourite expressions has always been: Science, art and poor folk – honour these and the people.

I hope that this book would serve as an inspiration for similar books in other countries because people all over the world have a lot to offer each other and there are plenty other innovations out there!

Apart from this book, I would also like to recommend Richard Wilkinson and Kate Pickett's work *The Spirit Level. Why Equality is Better for Everyone* (Penguin Books 2009).

I would like to extend my thanks to all the writers, my erstwhile parliamentary assistants Katri Söder and Olga Boustani (née Borovkova), and the producers of the first edition of the book Pilvi Riikka Taipale and Joonas Luotonen.

This book was a whole lot of fun to make!

Ilkka Taipale (editor) M.D., Ph.D.

CONTENTS

Foreword of the second edition by President Sauli Niinistö
Foreword of the first edition by President Tarja Halonen
Introduction by Editor Ilkka Taipale

ADMINISTRATION

1 Single-Chamber Parliament – Riitta Uosukainen ... 16
2 Constitutional Law Committee – Jarmo Vuorinen ... 20
3 Committee for the Future – Jyrki Katainen 24
4 Municipal Self-Governance – Pekka Nousiainen... 28
5 The Principle of Transparency – Lasse Lehtonen 31
6 Population Register – Hannu Luntiala 36
7 Coalition Governments – Harri Holkeri 41
8 Tripartism – Timo Kauppinen 44
9 Women's Suffrage and the 40 Percent Quota
 – Tuula Haatainen 47
10 No Corruption – Johannes Koskinen 50
11 Bilingualism – Göran von Bonsdorff 53
12 Åland – An Autonomous Region in Finland
 – Gunnar Jansson 56
13 Sámi People – Pekka Aikio 60

SOCIAL POLICY

14 Social Housing – Martti Lujanen 66
15 No Slums – Pekka Korpinen 70
16 Y-Foundation – Hannu Puttonen 72
17 Student Accommodation – Ulla-Mari Karhu 74
18 24-hour Service Homes – Ilkka Taipale 76
19 Status of the Romani Population – Kyösti Suonoja .. 80
20 Housing Company Model – Martti Lujanen 84

21	Employment Pension Scheme – Kari Puro	88
22	Child Day Care – Vappu Taipale	91
23	Child home-Care Allowance – Marjatta Väänänen	94
24	Paternity Leave – Johannes Koskinen	98
25	Maternity Pack – Sirpa Taskinen	101
26	Free School Meals – Kirsi Lindroos	104
27	Caring for Disabled War Veterans – Veli-Matti Huittinen	107
28	Abilis Foundation – Kalle Könkkölä	111
29	Caregivers Allowance – Päivi Voutilainen & Reija Heinola	116
30	Combating Poverty – Matti Heikkilä	119
31	Quarantee Foundation – Leena Veikkola	122
32	Social Credit – Marianne Rikama	125
33	State Alcohol Monopoly – Jussi Simpura	127
34	November Movement – Ilkka Taipale	130
35	Three Percent Theory – Ilkka Taipale	134
36	Legal Aid and Criminal Damage Compensation – Tuija Brax	137
37	Victim–Offender Mediation in Criminal Matters – Juhani Iivari	140

HEALTH

38	All-Inclusive Health Centres – Simo Kokko	144
39	Maternity and Well-Baby Clinics – Marjukka Mäkelä	148
40	Finnish Student Health Service – Vesa Vuorenkoski	151
41	The Finnish Institute of Occupational Health	154
42	Halving the Number of Road Deaths – Pekka Tarjanne	157

43	The North Karelia Project – Pekka Puska	160
44	Schizophrenia Project – Yrjö O. Alanen	164
45	National Suicide Prevention Project – Jouko Lönnqvist	168
46	Controlling Sexually Transmitted Infections – Osmo Kontula	170
47	Tobacco Legislation and Legal Actions – Mervi Hara	173
48	Xylitol – Marjatta Sandström	179

CULTURE

49	The Finnish Literature Society – Tuomas M. S. Lehtonen	182
50	Finno-Ugrian Society – Riho Grünthal	185
51	Finnish Libraries – Kaarina Dromberg	189
52	Finnish Comprehensive Schools – Erkki Aho	192
53	Free Education – Sonja Kosunen	195
54	Literacy of Finnish Children – Jukka Sarjala	198
55	University Decentralisation – Jaakko Numminen	201
56	Student Grants – Elina Karjalainen	204
57	Music Schools – Minna Lintonen	206
58	Non-Formal Adult Education – Jyrki Ijäs	208
59	Figurenote Method – Machiko Yamada	212
60	Storycrafting Method – Monika Riihelä	215

REGIONAL

61	Nordic Co-Operation – Larserik Maggman	220
62	The Northern Dimension – Paavo Lipponen	222
63	Tornio Haparanda Twin City – Hannes Manninen	226

64	Sponsor Commune Movement – Aura Korppi-Tommola	231
65	Demilitarised Åland – Roger Jansson	234
66	The Resettlement of Karelians – Hannu Kilpeläinen	238
67	Finnish Non-Violent Resistance – Steve Huxley	242

CIVIL SOCIETY

68	The Promised Land of NGOs – Risto Alapuro & Martti Siisiäinen	246
69	Road Maintenance Association	250
70	Finland's Slot Machine Association – Markku Ruohonen	254
71	Unionisation – Mikko Mäenpää	257
72	Party Subsidies – Risto Salonen	260
73	Economic Autonomy of Student Unions – Linnea Meder	263
74	The Coalition of Finnish Women's Associations – Tanja Auvinen	267
75	The Service Centre for Development Cooperation – Folke Sundman	270
76	One Percent for Global Solidarity – Thomas Wallgren	273
77	Peace Station – Kalevi Suomela	277
78	Prometheus Camps and the Youth Philosophy Event – Matti Mäkelä	281
79	Common Responsiblity Campaign – Kalle Kuusimäki	284
80	Operation Hunger Day Campaign – Hannu-Pekka Laiho	287

HI-TECH

81 Linux – Jyrki J. J. Kasvi 292
82 SMS Messaging – Matti Makkonen 295
83 IRC (Internet Relay Chat) – Jarkko Oikarinen 298
84 The Molotov Cocktail – Heikki Koski 300

EVERYDAY AMUSEMENT

85 Working Bees – Reino Hjerppe 304
86 Sauna – Lasse Viinikka 306
87 Santa Claus – Juha Nirkko 308
88 Seurasaari Christmas Path
    – Marjaliisa Kauppinen 312
89 Finnish Tango – Pekka Jalkanen 315
90 Everyman's Right – Juha Korkeaoja 319
91 Eroticism in Everyday Life
    – Elina Haavio-Mannila 322
92 Ice-Fishing – Kari Rajamäki 326
93 Ice Swimming – Paula Kokkonen 329
94 Pesäpallo – Finland's National Sport
    – Markku Pullinen 333
95 Nordic Walking – Eero Akaan-Penttilä 336
96 Dish Drying Cabinet – Pirkko Kasanen 339
97 Public Laundering Jetties
    – Pirkko Ruuskanen-Parrukoski 342
98 Dry Toilets – Asta Rajala 345
99 'Mad' Jokes – Jussi Särkelä 347
100 Star of Africa – Kari Mannerla 349

ADMINISTRATION

1 SINGLE-CHAMBER PARLIAMENT

At first I was astonished: how on Earth could the single-chamber parliament be a social innovation along with, say, liquorice and tobacco legislation? Then I understood: it is in fact the mother of all the innovations in this book. At least, this is my opinion, writing as someone who, as Finland's first female Speaker, has presided over no fewer than nine parliamentary sessions and who places a high premium on our parliamentary system.

In 1906 the Diet enacted the Election Act and the Parliament Act for Finland, and Finland made the transition from Europe's most primitive system of representation, based on four estates, to what many considered the most modern: a single-chamber parliament. The new Parliament Act, which came into force on 1 October 1906, established universal and equal suffrage. What was significant was that women were enfranchised at the same time as men; every Finnish citizen aged 24 or over was entitled to vote, and the number of people entitled to vote and stand for election increased tenfold overnight to 1.2 million.

It is often claimed that Finnish women were not first in this respect, as their counterparts in the Isle of Man, New Zealand, Australia and in some of the American states had been granted the right to vote at an earlier date, and in some cases were also allowed to stand for election, but no women were elected. Thus, in 1907, the world's first female mps took their seats in the Finnish Parliament. The fact that men and women achieved these rights at the same time was both a strength and particularity of Finland.

All these events took place in the Grand Duchy of Finland during a time of Tsarist oppression when a window of opportunity suddenly opened up: confronted with Russia's bad fortunes in the war with Japan, including the Tsusima sea battle, and other problems like the general strike which affected all social classes, also in Finland, the tsar approved the new Parliament Act.

Even though the prevailing conditions had an impact, it must be stressed that Finns had already done serious parliamentary groundwork, although the political party system was undeveloped and wise opinions were needed. Leo Mechelin's statesmanship was a godsend, and men and women worked hard. There were more than enough problems: debates raged about a single-chamber parliament, the Finnish and Swedish languages, illegal conscription and, later, the possibility of a monarchist Finland. A decision was eventually taken to form a single-chamber parliament, and the Grand Committee assumed the role of a kind of upper house. The Grand Committee later started attending to Eu-ropean Union matters in a model fashion.

The Finnish Women's Association had the goal of universal suffrage, but this was somewhat unclear even among the association's members. The same situation prevailed in the Feminist Association unioni, although its first president Lucina Hagman had written a pamphlet on women's suffrage in 1889. The Working Women's Union, however, supported universal suffrage more specifically. The women's associations and the Working Women's Union had different emphases. The fight for universal suffrage and the temperance question were closely intertwined, and demands for a prohibitionary alcohol law and democracy were considered different aspects of the same theme. The idea of universal and equal suffrage thus gained a lot of currency among the population during the abstinence movement in 1898–1899.

In any case, the universal and equal right to vote and stand for election was accomplished, surprising even Finland's most internationally oriented female politician, Aleksandra Gripenberg, who received notice of the event in England. From that time onwards she never wasted an opportunity to remind her audience that the eyes of the world were on Finnish women, who had in a unique fashion accomplished opportunities to act. There was an urgent need for education because women were obliged to appeal to the State for gender-based exemptions in order to achieve positions of power or receive higher education. Prostitution and other moral issues were also topical questions; all the women's groups were up their eyes in work. They worked together with the men, but were also derided because of their looks, spinsterhood, corpulence etc. – in much the same way as they are today.

In 2007 we have good reason to celebrate our accomplishments, although there is still much work to be done. Matters concerning family legislation, women's wages and reproduction are still discussed in the media. On the other hand, Finnish women have achieved top positions in Finnish politics: the first female President of the Republic was elected in 2000, the first female Speaker of Parliament in 1994, and the first Prime Minister in 2003. There are numerous brilliant women in business and politics, so breakthroughs have been accomplished in many sectors. Nevertheless, there are more than enough grievances.

Sometimes one hardly knows whether to laugh or cry when one looks at the matters currently under discussion in Parliament. Already in November 1907, *Koti ja Yhteiskunta* magazine reported that, thanks to women's joint endeavours, Parliament had decided to abolish prostitution, but our parliament is currently discussing the buying and selling of sexual services. In the first elections, some women believed that their vote could eradicate drinking from Finland forever, but there is still a heated debate about alcohol in the 21st century.

All things considered, we have to congratulate the wise statesmen and stateswomen of the turn of the 20th century. A single-chamber parliament was a suitable arrangement for Finland. Let it now work for it's own joy and for the honour of the land of our fathers.

We have rejoiced at the success achieved by Finnish Members of Parliament, be they men or women. In 1907, Members of the Russian Duma united to praise Finnish women in telegrams, including one from the Cossacks of the Don: "We, the representatives of the Cossacks of the Don, are fortunate to be able to salute the nation that has awarded women the high position they deserve in our great but still enchained native land. Long live the Finnish woman, who enjoys full rights as a citizen of her native land!"

Riitta Uosukainen – Councelor of State,
Speaker of Parliament 1994–2003

2 CONSTITUTIONAL LAW COMMITTEE

Finland has no constitutional court, but the constitutionality of new laws is deliberated during their enactment by the Constitutional Law Committee, which is one of the Finnish Parliament's (innovation no. 1) fifteen special committees. It became a permanent body in the parliamentary reform of 1906. The main task of the special committees is to prepare matters for decision-making in plenary sessions.

The Constitutional Law Committee prepares matters for plenary sessions related to enacting, amending or abolishing constitutional laws. The Committee also prepares matters pertaining to legislation closely related to constitutional laws. These include election laws, legislation concerning the highest organs of government, and matters involving the self-government of the Åland Islands (innovation no. 12), citizenship, language (innovation no. 11) and political parties (innovation no. 72).

The composition of reports to plenary has however been only a secondary function of the Committee during recent electoral periods; it is currently mainly concerned with issuing statements on matters prepared in other special committees. The number of statements issued has increased during the time of the last government: in 1999–

2002 the committee gave 199 statements compared to 167 in 2007–2010 and only 51 in 1987–1990.

According to section 74 of the Finnish Constitution, "the Constitutional Law Committee shall issue statements on the constitutionality of legislative proposals and other matters brought for its consideration, as well as on their relation to international human rights treaties." In addition, section 38 of the Finnish Parliament's Rules of Procedure state that "if, in respect to a legislative proposal or another matter under preparation in a committee, a question arises concerning its constitutionality or relation to human rights treaties, the committee shall request a statement on the matter from the Constitutional Law Committee." These provisions provide a systematic framework for the constitutional control of matters debated in Parliament. The particularity of this Finnish system is that constitutional control is anticipatory and is executed by an organ elected by Parliament from among its own members. This particularity can be explained by the fact that the system was created 150 years ago.

In executing constitutional control the Committee functions as a judicial organ which interprets the constitution, and it executes a similar "apolitical" role when it delivers its report to plenary sessions on e.g. the illegality of a minister's procedure or the judicial preconditions for the dismissal of an mp. Regardless of these kinds of judicial functions, the Committee's composition is similar to all other special committees in that it represents the parliamentary balance of power.

The impartiality of the Constitutional Law Committee in judicial matters within its jurisdiction is ensured by several factors. In matters related to the Constitutional Law Committee's judicial interpretations, parliamentary factions do not make group decisions that the committee members would have to follow. Neither do ministers attempt to affect the independence of Committee members' actions. Discretion on constitutional matters is truly left to members of the Constitutional Law Committee. The Committee tries to make its actions consistent with its previous decisions.

In each separate matter regarding constitutional interpretation, the Committee listens to several constitutional law experts from different universities to help them reach a decision. The experts present a review of the Committee's interpretation policy and their own well-founded recommendations on how to interpret the constitution with regards to the matter in question.

The experts' opinions are seldom identical in all respects. The Committee does not necessarily adopt the majority opinion, but on the other hand it cannot really disagree with a unanimous group. The experts' recommendations and arguments provide the Committee members with a certain kind of framework for their own opinions. These are later debated and developed in Committee meetings, and the vast majority of recent statements have been unanimous. However, should a member be of a different opinion, he or she has the right to include a minority report in the Committee's statement.

In its statement the Committee presents e.g. an evaluation of the constitutionality of a legislative proposal. If it considers the proposal to be in conflict with the Constitution, the statement includes indications on how the proposal should be amended to guarantee its constitutionality. The amendments suggested by the Committee do not have the form of an Act, but they describe the objective of the amendment and possibly include an example of how that objective could be achieved. In practise, the other special committees comply with the Committee's observations. Ultimately, it is the responsibility of the Speaker of the Parliament to ensure that plenary debate on the matter complies with the Constitution.

Generally speaking, the Committee enjoys full confidence in the propriety of its constitutional interpretations. Any lack of confidence would be problematic because the anticipatory control executed by the Committee was for a long time the only form of constitutional legal control. In accordance with the Finnish Constitution, which was established in 1919, the analysis of the constitutionality of laws was not within the jurisdiction of the judicial courts, although this situation later changed. Section 106 of the new Finnish Constitution states that "If, in a matter being tried by a court of law, the application of an Act would be in apparent conflict with the Constitution, the court shall give precedence to the provision in the Constitution."

The success of the Constitutional Law Committee's constitutional control is illustrated by the fact that, during the first six years of the new Finnish Constitution, there has been only few cases in which a court of law has given precedence to the Constitution in respect of the provision of an Act.

Jarmo Vuorinen – Deputy secretary general of the Finnish parliament

3 COMMITTEE FOR THE FUTURE

Parliamentary power in every country can be divided between legislative power and budget power, but the Finnish Parliament (innovation no. 1) has the unique character of possessing a kind of visionary power too, for which a special committee was founded approximately 20 years ago: the Committee for the Future. It is still the only committee in the world in which mps focus on matters related to the future, although in some countries the more limited one of its two tasks – the evaluation of the consequences of technological development for society – has been assigned to a parliamentary committee (generally a committee for science and technology).

A constitutional reform in 2000 consolidated the Committee for the Future as a permanent committee comparable to Parliament's other special committees. The persistence of mps was a deciding factor in the development of this institution. The initiative for organising parliamentary debate on the future and for creating a forum for comprehensive future policies was taken by the Parliament. A parliamentary majority made sure that the proposition was carried in spite of opposition, but it took several years.

Already in 1986, a total of 133 mps out of 200 signed their names to a proposal regarding the foundation of a future studies unit as part of the legislative body. This was discussed as a written question, but it did not result in concrete action. The debate continued, and 166 Members of Parliament formulated a legislative proposal on the matter in 1992, but that also failed. The most eager mps at that time were Eero Paloheimo and Martti Tiuri, who became the first presidents of the Committee when it was eventually founded. Even though the legislative proposal failed to succeed, the Constitutional Law Committee stated that Finland had a clear need for futures policies and dialogue between the government and Parliament concerning long-term problems and options.

In 1992 the Committee was of the opinion that the Government should produce a report on future development for Parliament, i.e. a comprehensive study, based on futures studies' methods, on essential matters concerning social development and alternative future developments. In addition, the Government would state objectives, according to which society would be developed. Parliament decided to appoint this task to the Government, and a committee was formed to discuss the Government's report on the long-term future. The committee was named the Committee for the Future.

According to the current stipulations, "The Committee for the Future considers parliamentary documents referred to it and, when requested to do so, makes submissions to other committees on futures-related matters, which are included in their spheres of responsibility and have a bearing on development factors and development models of the future. The Committee conducts research associated with futures studies, including methodology, and it also functions as a parliamentary body that conducts assessments of technological developments and the impact of technology on society. The Committee has a small annual budget, which allows it to commission external reports and studies. The main task of the Committee for the Future is to review the Government's white paper on the future and prepare a statement on it for Parliament, but it is also in charge of evaluating the consequences of technological development for society.

The autonomy initially given to the Committee has been strengthened over the years. It chooses a few major social issues related to the future at the beginning of each electoral period, and then produces a report on these in cooperation with other bodies. Some of these reports are then discussed in plenary sessions. Reports include "Challenges of the Global Information Society", which was produced in cooperation with philosopher Pekka Himanen, and "The Future of Health Care", which was produced in cooperation with a health research group from the University of Kuopio and futures researcher Osmo Kuusi.

The Committee has also conducted research on regional innovative environments and social capital. The reports have been widely discussed in the media, and the debate still continues.

During the 20 years since it was founded, the Committee has during each electoral period focused on themes which are highly relevant to Finnish society, such as globalisation, new technologies, knowledge management, and innovations. During the last electoral period, it produced, in cooperation with the futures studies specialist Mika Mannermaa, a Finnish survey on democracy entitled "Democracy in the Turmoil of the Future". This was published in 2007. In 2006, as part of the Centenary of the Parliament of Finland celebrations, the Committee published "Democracy and Futures", a compilation of articles on democracy in 2100 by international futures studies specialists.

The Committee for the Future has consolidated its position. It has drawn plenty of attention and spawned successors in various forms.

*Jyrki Katainen – Prime Minister, Chairman
of the committee for the future 2003–2007*

4 MUNICIPAL SELF-GOVERNANCE

In accordance with the Constitution, Finland is divided into municipalities, whose administration is based on the self-government of their residents. The decision-making power of local authorities is exercised by a council elected by the residents. Provisions on the general principles governing municipal administration and the municipalities' duties are set out in an Act. Additionally, the municipalities have the right to levy municipal tax. Municipalities in Finland have wide-ranging powers. In accordance with the Local Government Act, local authorities perform the functions that they are responsible for by virtue of their autonomy and those they are required to do by law. In other words, functions that are common and important to residents and which are not performed by other authorities. Local authorities can be allocated or deprived of functions or rights by legislation passed to this effect. Those functions constitute the municipality's specific sphere of authority. Extensive functions that fall within the specific sphere of authority include education, health care and extensive social welfare services. Furthermore, the municipalities are responsible for matters related to the residents' free-time, recreation, housing, and the management and maintenance of their living environment (i.e. roads, streets, water supply and sewerage), as well as land-use planning and functional municipal structures.

One of the most essential functions of the municipality is to provide adequate and quality services for its residents. It must also ensure the vitality of the area, i.e. secure a good environment and promote the development of entrepreneurship and the creation of employment.

Tax revenues have a critical role in municipal finances. The power to levy and collect taxes is one of the cornerstones of municipal self-governance as it ensures that the municipalities can manage the functions that they have undertaken to execute or that they are responsible for by law. The most important is municipal tax, which amounts to almost 13 billion euros. Corporate income tax amounts to a little over 1 billion euros, and real estate tax also raises almost 1 billion euros annually. The municipalities must have as wide a tax base as possible, also in the future, because it enables municipal self-governance as it is designated in the law and ensures that not all municipal resources are used performing their legal requirements.

The Finnish municipalities are naturally very diverse, and conditions vary in different parts of this extensive country. The State must therefore have the necessary means to even out disparities in municipal incomes to give residents equal access to adequate basic services irrespective of the size or location of their municipality. One of the central constitutional principles regarding municipal self-governance is that, when allocating new functions to municipalities, the State must also to ensure that they have the necessary resources to carry them out. Finland must therefore have a well-functioning relationship between the

State and the local authorities, as well as a state-subsidy system which ensures municipal resources and residents' equal access to services.

Pekka Nousiainen – Member of Parliament 1999–2007, President of the Finnish local and regional authorities 2003–2009, Council chairman 2009–

5 THE PRINCIPLE OF TRANSPARENCY

Finland is an open and democratic society. According to Section 21 under the Constitution of Finland provisions concerning the transparency of proceedings, the right to be heard, the right to receive a reasoned decision and the right of appeal, as well as other guarantees of a fair trial and good governance, are laid down in an act.

The so-called principle of transparency is often regarded as a Swedish institution, but it is in fact part of Finland's common history with Sweden. One of the people who formulated the principle was the Finn Anders Chydenius, who represented the Ostrobothnian clergy in the Swedish parliament during the 1760s. The Swedish state was in crisis during the first half of the 18th century. Having lost two wars against Russia, the broad spread of corruption threatened the very existence of the whole state. At the same time the philosophy of the age of the enlightenment championed devolving more power to the people and greater control of those in power (e.g. the separation of powers inherent in Montesquieu's tripartite system). The ability of the parliament that consisted of the four estates to monitor The use of power was very limited, however. The estates met rarely and they didn't receive information about the government's decisions. Apart from this, censorship limited political discussion. The idea of freedom of information thus gained wide support especially amongst estates other than the nobility in the 1750s.

Anders Chydenius was especially active in 1765–66 in lobbying for the freedom of information. The eventual Freedom of Information Act followed very closely the views put forward by Chydenius in his memos and other writings. In 1766 the parliament accepted the Freedom of Information Act and it became a part of the constitution. This law stated that "everyone has the right to access government documents and make copies of them". The Freedom of Information Act guaranteed Swedes and Finns a wider freedom to publish than existed anywhere else. Additionally, almost all government documents became open to the public. This was an unforseen innovation in monitoring government activity.

The constitution from the Swedish state remained in force in Finland when the country came under Russian control in 1809. When Finland became independent in 1917 the principle of transparency became part of the legislation regarding the freedom to publish. Nowadays the principle is very detailed and part of the act that governs the transparency of government activity. According to section one of this act, documents produced by civil servants are public if not legally decreed otherwise.

The demand that limits on accessing official documents have to be legislated in parliamentary law is there to guarantee that any limitations on publicity are unavoidable and based on reasons that the majority of the population would be ready to accept. This also guarantees that the mere embarrassing nature of certain information from the perspective of a single civil servant or a ministry is not enough to stop information entering the public sphere.

Furthermore, publicity helps ensure that civil servants work efficiently and official procedures are not tainted by favouritism or discrimination. In many surveys Finland has been named as one of the world's least corrupt countries.

Also in Finland the Freedom of Information Act and related laws state that not all government information is open to the public. The reason for secrecy may be public interest (e.g. state security, crime prevention) or private interest (e.g. to protect children or protect private life). Many official decisions that affect individual people are however open in Finland. For instance, information about what people have paid in taxes along with their taxable income is in the public domain, and the information always ends up in the tabloids.

The law on freedom of information requires that if a public official refuses to give government documents to a citizen, a formal, written decision must be delivered including the grounds for the refusal. This kind of administrative decision can be appealed in the administration court, where the matter is settled by an independent court. The openness of official documents in Finland is monitored efficiently through the justice system.

The Finnish media also closely monitors how the principle of transparency is being executed in practice. Attempts by government officials to prevent media access to information easily leads to courtroom appeals and negative stories in the press. The courts have in recent years granted access to e.g. an individual civil servants' expenses and taxi journey reimbursements and how well different high schools did in the final exams, but on the other hand a list of names retrieved from foreign intelligence sources by the Finnish security intelligence service regarding possible collaboration between Finnish informers and the former GDR security police has remained a secret even after a court case.

The principle of transparency has a number of functions in Finland's political life too. It guarantees everyone a right to access information, and thus promotes equality among citizens with regards to the information society that we live in. The principle of transparency ensures transparent government. Open government is part of the preemptive guarantee of justice, i.e. it promotes a good quality of government decision-making and ensures that justice is fairly served. The principle of transparency enables citizens to efficiently control government and makes it easier for people to effect change. It promotes the free formation of opinion and helps democracy flourish in practical terms, and it also promotes the high quality of the media. With regards to the current information age, the principle of transparency is also linked to the demand for civil servants to follow a good governance of information as they execute their duties. Civil servants have to take care of documents and information systems and the accessibility, usability, completeness and protection of the information that they contain, along with other factors that influence the quality of the information. It does not thus suffice that the information is provided on request, rather civil servants must ensure that it is genuinely accessible to everyone. Civil servants' different files must also form a clear system which enables citizens to find the information they are looking for.

The principle of transparency has been adapted to suit different kinds of places and has spread from Sweden and Finland to other places in the world. For example, in 1966 the USA accepted the freedom of information act (FOIA) and, according to Wikipedia, there are similar laws in 85 other countries. Sweden and Finland have also demanded that the principle of transparency be followed in the European Union. The Treaty of Amsterdam, which amended the treaty that established the European Union, included an article on the public availability of official documents. Based on this article the European Parliament and Council passed an act on access to documents (ey n:o 1049/2001) which rules that the public has an access to the documents produced by the European Parliament, Council and Commission. In this way the principle of transparency has become part of general European legislation.

Lasse Lehtonen, Administrative chief physician,
Hospital district of Helsinki and Uusimaa

 POPULATION REGISTER

Finland began to keep a register of all the country's inhabitants in the 16th century already, with the Finnish church and state beginning the practice around the same time.

The main motive of this for the state was to facilitate taxation and conscription. The Swedish-Finnish state was at that time a very sparsely-populated and poor country, so the maintenance of an extensive administrative and military organization necessitated information about the "conscriptable population" and tax-liable citizens and their property.

Information about people and their property started to be collected in separate and continuously-updated documents. The population register was born of the documents on people, while the documents on property evolved into register on property ownership.

Parallel to the population register was the register that was kept by the Lutheran church, which was inspired by the need to save souls. The register on the one hand included congregation lists and on the other hand monitored church activities and related events. The result of all this was comprehensive documentation that also included family relationships. The registers that the church kept had sufficient information about population changes and family relationships, so the state's registers didn't concern itself with such details.

When a dependable and comprehensive census for the whole country was deemed necessary in the 18th century, the state was unwilling to pay for the costs of collecting the basic information. Congregations were thus charged with contributing information about their local register to state officials from the Department of Statistics. The earliest census statistics were thus gathered on the basis of church registers. This created a foundation for a more comprehensive population census in later years.

The population register in Swedish Finland was not the first project of its kind in the world: similar lists had been compiled hundreds if not thousands of years ago in Egypt and China, while in the western hemisphere the most famous was perhaps the tax-collection drive that Emperor Augustus ordered, and which is mentioned in the New Testament.

However, the register that began in Swedish Finland is unique because of its continuity. Having begun in the mid-16th century it has continued without a break until the present day.

Old population registers that have been compiled by the church and the state have been preserved for later generations, and the data is a rich source of information for researchers. Old population registers have yielded unique information to help e.g. genealogy researchers as well as medical studies.

The ongoing registration of details for the local population register survived unchanged for a long time. Manual transcription of the register, which had been the way for centuries, began to be computerised in the 1970s, and at this time the local registers that had been maintained separately by the church and the state were combined for the first time.

Since then, information about residents of Finland has been available to the authorities at the touch of a button through the National Population Information System.

Over the last forty years the methods of collecting the information have been constantly improved. While information was earlier collected with the help of forms which took several weeks to register, nowadays most of the information in Finland's National Population Information System can be transferred electronically from other civil servants. Information is registered very fast: new details reach the register within days.

The information is also used more widely. The population register was originally established to serve the needs of national and local government, especially with regards to taxation and conscription, but in recent decades the system has been increasingly used in the business world. Nowadays in Finland over half of the usage of the population register caters for the business world's needs. The most important use is however still in serving national and local government.

The broad use of the National Population Information System is also a guarantee of quality. When the information is used, mistakes are revealed and can then be fixed. Finland's National Population Information System is among the best in the world in terms of comprehensiveness and quality.

Every country constructs a population register according to its own needs and opportunities. A system that suits one country will not necessarily suit another. In the development of the population register it is necessary to take many factors into account: the country's economic and technological possibilities, history, laws, values and culture.

In Finland the information content in the electronic National Population Information System is impressive. The system contains important and current information about every citizen. The most important information is the person's name, date and place of birth and their nationality. Information about their family relationships (spouse, children and parents) and street address are also important.

Every person in Finland has an identity number that has been created by the National Population Information System, and this means that people with the same name or the same date of birth can be differentiated from each other. The identity number is registered in the National Population Information System and is widely used in all kinds of national information systems. This identification number makes it possible to use registers efficiently. The use of this identification requires strict adherence to the principles of data protection.

An up-do-date population register makes it possible to take care of many societal matters in a reliable and efficient manner. For example, the register makes it cheaper to compile statistics and take care of elections, taxation and the distribution of benefits. Using the system also reduces the amount of bureaucracy. When officials retrieve information about individuals from the reliable electronic population register, people themselves carry less of an administrative burden as they do not have to provide information to different authorities over and over again.

Every country in the world carries out a regular census. The purpose of this is to gather reliable information about the country's citizens and their living conditions. In most countries the information is collected every 5 or 10 years.

Usually data for the census is collected in such a way that a specific organization is created to plan the forms and collect the information face-to-face and then record and store and turn the massive data bank into statistics.

Censuses in Finland have been carried out recently every 20 years in a way that the information is collected directly from the existing information system, so it is never necessary to ask citizens to provide information in forms. The register-based census that is carried out in Finland costs a fraction of what traditional manual collection costs in other countries. Additionally, the information can be quickly accessed when required.

A broad and detailed population register is an important base for many functions in every country. As the register holds important personal information it is important that it is safeguarded from inappropriate use. For this reason a data protection system must be well enforced to keep the data safe.

Data protection principles are encoded in the law. It is also important that use of the information can be monitored. As it would be a huge problem if the information was to fall into the wrong hands, the safety of the information is not just guarded legally but also in many other practical ways such as information technology which prevents unauthorized use.

Hannu Luntiala – Director of Population Register Centre

7 COALITION GOVERNMENTS

In the beginning of 20th century the Grand Duchy of Finland shifted from a diet of four estates to a democratic parliament (innovation no. 1), and new provisions were enacted for universal and equal parliamentary elections. With regards to women's suffrage (innovation no. 9), for example, Finland went further than any other country, but having said that the general models and elements of electoral legislation were adopted from abroad.

It would be interesting to analyse how important it was that the central figures of the public law elite and scholars of constitutional law, such as K.J. Ståhlberg and Robert Hermannson, had adopted their perceptions mainly from St. Petersburg. In the European context, they were more orientated towards the continental German-French way of thinking than the Anglo-Saxon political system. According to tradition, this orientation was greatly influenced by the language skills they had developed in the course of their education.

The most decisive factor was to opt for proportional representation, a mode of election that has persisted and consolidated our multiparty system. The British "winner-takes-all" system with electoral constituencies in which each party only fields one candidate would have resulted in a completely different combination of political parties.

Party politics have naturally changed with the times over the centuries, but they have a relatively stable base and, consequently, a strong impact. No political party has had an absolute majority in the Finnish Parliament since the country became independent. On the other hand the parliamentary principle is written into the Constitution in that it is stated that the government must have the confidence of the majority of the parliament. The governing parties have therefore always had to cooperate with other parties, and the occasional minority governments have needed allies in critical situations. The provisions relating to the stipulated majority have also been highly significant.

In earlier times it was common for governments to change. In the 1970s it was calculated that the average duration of a government in independent Finland was approximately one year, but during the last 25 years we have got used to majority governments that sit for the whole electoral period. Many of these coalitions have however been ideologically quite disconcerting.

Governmental responsibility has on occasions been jointly borne by two apparently opposite political movements, and populist parties have not been shunned as they have in other European countries. It might be said that an adequate dose of responsibility has had a surprisingly calming effect, however, for during the last decades there have been no well-organised, broad-based extremist movements in Finland.

In spring 1987 the President of Finland Mauno Koivisto appointed a coalition government based on the cooperation of the Social Democratic Party and the National Coalition Party. I will not evaluate its achievements and mistakes in this context, but with regards to Finnish political rules it prepared the way for a more democratic and parliamentary transparent government policy. Its mission was to demonstrate that party-political cooperation could be based on future visions instead of past experiences.

It has been almost nine decades since the Finnish Civil War, but its horrors still live in the collective memory of our nation. However, the desire to take care of our common matters has been stronger than any ideological divisions and has ensured the stable development of our country. Coalition governments are therefore a central part of Finnish political tradition and the essence of social action.

Harri Holkeri – Prime Minister 1987–1991

8 TRIPARTISM

Tripartism is the three-partner model upon which Finnish labour relations are based. Labour and capital, with their respective organisations are at opposite ends of the triangle's base line and the government is at the apex. This is tripartism's strategic triangle. This triangle forms the basis of negotiations between employers, employees and the government over economic, social and financial goals in the labour market. The outcome forms the Incomes Policy Agreement, based upon which sectoral unions negotiate and conclude collective and legally binding labour agreements, which may be adapted in specific workplaces to fit their needs.

The tripartism model was formed by the pressure of the Winter War in 1940, its rules being laid down in the "January Engagement", according to which, through active encouragement from the government (which acted as a match-maker in the engagement), employers conceded the right of unionisation and workers the right of employers to manage and distribute work.

The first tripartite agreement was concluded in 1945. The Confederation of Finnish Employers (STK) represented the employers, and the Confederation of Finnish Trade Unions (SAK) represented the workers. The

State acted as the agreement's guarantor through price and wage regulation laws.

The first experiences of tripartism were encouraging, but the agreement did not manage to guarantee real income development or peaceful labour relations during the years of post-war shortages. Despite its problems, however, the participants and the state were convinced of the usefulness of tripartism, especially when bilateral agreements in 1956-77 yielded poor results because they lacked grounding in the economic, labour and social politics that are typical of tripartism.

1968 saw a return to tripartism in the midst of high unemployment with the first collective Incomes Policy Agreement that comprehensively covered the entire society. Organisations representing blue and white-collar workers as well as academics on the one hand and employer organizations representing private and municipal employers and the state on the other hand all participated. In the 40 years that this endured it played a large role in Finland's development as a Nordic welfare state.

Demands regarding the flexibility of working life led to experimentation with a bipartite model between 2007–2011, but the results produced inflation and failed to suppor the ability to remain competitive on one hand and the goals of reducing unemployment on the other. Heavy pressure from the government in 2012 saw a return to tripartite negotiations and a two-year framework agreement was introduced: organizations that represent the employers agreed on the level of expenses and unions on pay rises on the basis of this agreement. Local adaptations may be negotiated in specific workplaces. The Finnish model is a three-level tripartite solution.

The Finnish model of tripartism has been very successful, taking into account employers' needs to improve international competitiveness, workers' needs for real income increases, and government demands for low unemployment and sustainable economic growth.

Tripartism has helped Finland rise to become one of the most competitive countries in the world, according to a World Economic Forum study, and European Commission statistics show that Finland is the leading country in IT innovations and applications. Education has also been developed successfully under the tripartite system, as can be seen from the agreements on education in working life and the OECD's PISA study, which puts Finnish pupils at the top of the class in reading and arithmetic. Tripartism must also be thanked for developing labour market and social policy legislation in particular and giving Finland a relatively equal income distribution and being the force behind progress in realising equal opportunities to the extent that Finland has become one of the world's leading welfare states in which, according to an EU comparative study, people see themselves as being happy.

Timo Kauppinen – European Foundation for the Improvement of Living & Working Condition Research Director 1999–2008

9 WOMEN'S SUFFRAGE AND THE 40 PERCENT QUOTA

The gender perspective should be taken into consideration in all decision-making, at all levels and at all stages. In the Beijing World Conference on Women in 1995, women's rights were declared human rights. If women do not have the opportunity to participate in decision-making, these rights cannot be fulfilled. The proportion of women in Finland who are involved the political decision-making process has increased promisingly, but the political sphere has long been divided into men's and women's sectors. Women's sectors were social affairs, health and education politics, but women have successfully worked in areas that have traditionally been considered male territory, such as the Prime Minister and the Ministries of Defence and Finance. In practice, women have proved themselves equally competent as decision-makers and experts. Our next objective is to increase the proportion of women involved in economic decision-making.

At the turn of the 20th century, the Finnish women's movement struggled for universal suffrage and the right to stand for election. Working-class women participated in organising the general strike of 1905, and a hundred years ago Finnish women won full political rights in public elections. At the same time, the Finnish system of representation was changed from a Diet of Four Estates into Europe's most democratic single-chamber parliament (innovation no. 1).

19 women were elected in the first parliamentary elections, almost a tenth of the total number of mps. Nine of them represented the Social Democrats and ten were from other parties.

Women have voted eagerly, and since 1991 they have been more active than men. Political power has been concentrating in Finnish women's hands; the nation voted Tarja Halonen into office as the first female President of the Republic of Finland in 2000, and backed her again in 2006. Riitta Uosukainen served as the first female Speaker of Parliament in 1994–2002, and Anneli Jäätteenmäki was appointed the first female Prime Minister in 2003.

The first female minister in Finland was Miina Sillanpää, who was appointed Minister for Social Affairs and Health in 1926. Women's proportion of ministerial posts rose to over 40% in Paavo Lipponen's second government (1999–1903), Anneli Jäätteenmäki's government (2003) and Matti Vanhanen's governments (2007–2012).

The proportion of female mps remained low for a long time. Between 1962–1991 it varied between 13.5 and 38.5%, and in the 2007 parliamentary elections 41,5% of those elected were women. The proportion of women taking part in elections has increased without quotas. The proportion of women elected in municipal elections has also increased; in the 2004 municipal elections approximately 37% of those elected to councils were women, and they received approximately 42% of the vote.

Gender quotas have been applied in Finland to indirectly elected government and municipal decision-making bodies since 1995. According to the general rule, equality requires at least 40% representation of both sexes. Gender balance is also mandatory in administrative boards and boards of directors in municipal or state-majority companies, as well as other governing or administrative bodies formed by elected officials. The current government has also increased the proportion of women when appointing boards of directors in state-owned companies. However, women have only marginal representation in economic decision-making. This matter requires attention in private companies too, for it would undoubtedly bring economic benefits.

Tuula Haatainen – Chair of the Council for Gender Equality (1995–2003), Minister of education (2003–2005), Minister of social affairs and health, Minister of equality (2005–2007)

10 NO CORRUPTION

Finland has enjoyed a leading position in the table of the world's least corrupt countries for many years: it was at number one in 2007 and has been in the top 6 since. Transparency International rates countries according to a survey that evaluates perceptions of the degree of corruption experienced by business people. Countries' legislation, law enforcement and judiciary systems are also analysed.

The research method might not give a full picture of every form of corruption, but it reveals the most essential; everyday bribery. The ratings reflect fairly well on contemporary lawmaking and enforcement, the functionality of governance, and the relevance of common rules to society.

There has been no controversy about the top marks awarded to Finland and the other Nordic countries. In addition to Finland, Iceland, Denmark, Sweden and Norway, the 2007 top ten least corrupted countries are New Zealand, Singapore, Switzerland, Holland and Canada.

One might wonder what our secret is, why Finland in particular has been so successful in eradicating corruption, and indeed this question is often asked at international gatherings by people from more distant cultural environments. On the other hand, in Europe our top rating seems to be somehow considered self-evident.

There are a number of objective, explanatory factors: transparent governance, the extensively applied principle of publicity, extensive municipal autonomy (innovation no. 4), a well-defined structure for the police force and judicial system, and a vigilant media which monitors how power is exercised and protects freedom of speech.

The transparency of public decision-making is the true cornerstone of anti-corruption measures because it enables the evaluation of decisions and their grounds. Part of the European Union's funding, for instance, is administered through non-public channels, which evokes constant mistrust.

The second fundamental element is the democracy of local government. Municipal power in Finland is in the hands of elected officials, and all minutes and decisions are entered into the public record, preventing corruption in e.g. decisions concerning town planning and construction contracts.

Another factor which enhances control over how power is exercised is that Finns are among the world's most eager newspaper subscribers and readers, especially when it comes to local papers. General education (innovation no. 52) and an exemplary library system (innovation no. 51) also promote control over the propriety of governance.

Other essential factors are the prevention of financial crimes through up-to-date legislation, adequately resourced tax audits, competent criminal investigations and an efficient judicial system. Finland's anti-bribery measures are prioritised both through education and the operations of the police, prosecutors and independent courts. Officials responsible for legal control, i.e. the Parliamentary Ombudsman and the Chancellor of Justice, are quick to get involved in complaints that include suspicions of corruption.

Following the discovery of widely covered-up election funding in Finland's 2007 parliamentary elections, the laws concerning election funding were tightened up considerably.

Obedience to the law in Finland has historical reasons. When Finland was an autonomous Grand Duchy from 1809–1917, the Swedish-Finnish judicial system was defended against Russian interference and periodic oppression. The integrity and strong morals of judges and public authorities were fundamental to this fight for legitimacy, and this strict principle of legality persisted during the development of independent Finland with regards to governance and control.

Johannes Koskinen – Minister of Justice 1999–2005, chairman of constitutional law committee 2011–

11 BILINGUALISM

Bilingualism is an important issue in Finland, a country with two official languages: Finnish and Swedish. Those who are fully bilingual can find good employment in national and municipal government as well as the private sector.

I have always considered myself bilingual, having Swedish as my mother tongue yet having been considered competent for a professorship at the University of Helsinki with Finnish as the teaching language. I might not know the Finnish names of some plant and animal species, but I am no naturalist, so I may be excused in making use of the Latin on occasion.

Add to this the fact that the language issue now seems to be of less significance than in my student days in the 1930s, when a disproportionate amount of leading positions were held by people whose mother tongue was Swedish. These days, the language requirement remains, but those concerned must blame themselves if they fail to meet it. There appears to be no discrimination based on mother tongue to speak of.

All this applies to people from wholly Finnish or Swedish-speaking households – people who have often expended blood, sweat and tears to learn the "second national language", nowadays more accurately referred to as the "first foreign language". But what is the situation for the genuinely bilingual – those who at home speak Finnish with one parent and Swedish with the other, and can think fluently in both languages?

In Belgium I have met people who define themselves as bilingual, and The Statesman's Yearbook has no accurate details on how many Belgians have French or Flemish as their first language. This does not apply in Finland. Here, all citizens must be registered from birth as either Finnish- or Swedish-speakers. So what do the genuinely bilingual do?

Professor of Statistics Gunnar Fougstedt discussed this matter in his 1955 book Social Factors Affecting the Choice of Language. He concluded that the choice of first language was mainly influenced by three factors: the mother's language, the language of schooling and the surrounding language. In addition there were a few other factors and naturally some exceptions to the rule.

Thus, if your mother is Finnish-speaking and you go to school in Kuopio, you are most likely to be registered as a Finnish-speaker – just as likely as you are to register as a Swedish-speaker if your mother speaks Swedish and you go to school in Ekenäs. Against this background, it is easy to understand why there are many young men with Swedish names and surnames who prefer to speak Finnish, and many young ladies with Finnish names and surnames who favour Swedish.

How will the situation develop in the future? Marriages that transcend language boundaries (I dislike the term "mixed marriages") seem to be increasing, but they do not necessarily imply an automatic choice of Finnish as the main language. I have often gently pointed out that while my grandfather was actually a Fennoman (a movement promoting the elevation of the Finnish language and culture), just one century ago my father leaned more towards the Constitutionalists, joining the Swedish People's Party. Politics was thus a strong factor.

Another perspective is that the environment is changing due to the increasing migration of Finnish-speakers to southern Finland. Naturally this is to the benefit of the Finnish language. On the other hand, the fact that the environment is becoming more Finnish may contribute to parents putting their children in Swedish language immersion programmes or Swedish schools to maintain bilingualism. So these two factors may actually partly balance each other out.

Finally, we should consider how ongoing globalisation affects bilingualism. It is hard to say; most of all, globalisation contributes to improving English skills among young people. In this way it can increase the facility for acquiring new languages: learning one foreign language makes it ever easier to learn others.

Is it therefore easier for Swedish-speakers than Finnish-speakers to become fluent in foreign tongues? Most probably yes, in the case of English and German, but generally speaking the most important factor is the attitude towards learning languages. Bilingualism will continue to be a good starting point for positive human contacts.

Göran von Bonsdorff – Professor emeritus

12 ÅLAND – AN AUTONOMOUS REGION IN FINLAND

The Åland Islands and its Swedish-speaking population have a rather special legal status in that they are autonomous under the sovereignty of Finland. Åland has enjoyed this status, which is well anchored in international law, for more than 80 years, but being somehow 'special' can also entail a lack of stability in the changing circumstances of post-Cold War Europe. For this reason the islanders hope that Europe will come to regard autonomous regions as being protected by EU law.

The Åland Islands are located between the Finnish and Swedish mainland, in the northern Baltic Sea at the entrance to the Gulf of Bothnia. Åland's combined land and sea area totals 6,784 kilometre. Almost 80% of this area is water, while the remaining 1,550 km^2 is comprised of approximately 6,500 islands and skerries, of which around 80 are inhabited throughout the year.

Åland currently has about 26,000 inhabitants, of which nearly 94% speak Swedish as their mother tongue (innovation no. 11).

During the last 600 years Åland has been subjected to the rule of external powers, with outsiders deciding what was best for it. Sweden ruled Finland until the beginning of the 19th century, during which time Åland, for administrative purposes, was part of Finland. The Swedish era ended when Russia took over in 1809.

Russian rule endured until 1917. During that period Åland, as part of the autonomous Grand Duchy of Finland under Russia, remained Swedish-speaking with its own culture and even economic structure.

The so-called Åland Islands Question was born amidst the turmoil of the end of World War I, mainly as a result of the American president Wilson's doctrine of people's right to self-determination. Even before Finland's declaration of independence in December 1917 a secession movement in Åland wanted the islands to reunite with Sweden. They were worried about the state of confusion in Russia and were fearful of strong Finnish dominance which might threaten the Swedish language and culture, and it also seemed possible that an independent Finland might become communist.

Scared of losing the islands completely, the Finnish Parliament hastily passed the Åland Autonomy Act in May 1920 without consulting those who lived there, but the islanders rejected the law and refused to recognise it, creating a considerable amount of tension between Finland and Sweden.

On an initiative by the United Kingdom the dispute was ultimately referred to the newly founded League of Nations, whose decision in June 1921 showed the Wisdom of Solomon by offering something to everybody:

1. Finland got sovereignty over Åland
2. the islanders were granted autonomy
3. Sweden was happy to see it demilitarized and declared neutral (innovation no. 65).

Today the Åland Islanders are living under the third Autonomy Act (the first was in force 1920–1951, the second 1952–1992 and the previous one was enacted in 1993), the reform of which is currently under discussion again in the region. The difference compared with the past is that the islanders themselves are now taking part and trying to master their own destiny in a democratic society ruled by law.

The Åland Autonomy Act cannot be amended by the Finnish Parliament without the consent of the Legislative Assembly of Åland, which has exclusive legislative power over the area. International treaties signed and ratified by Finland which affect the autonomous region must be approved by the Assembly before they can become law in Åland.

Administration is divided between the central official powers of Finland and the government of Åland along the same lines as the legislative power.

The law is enforced in Åland by state courts, as provided for by state legislation.

The inhabitants of Åland enjoy a special regional citizenship, called the right of domicile, which grants special economic and political rights to its holders and exempts them from military service and, in practice, from conscription altogether.

Since 1970 Åland has been a member of the Nordic Council, with the right to participate in both the Parliamentary Assembly and the Council of Ministers. When Finland (finally) joined the Council of Europe in 1989 the Legislative Assembly of Åland gave its approval, which means that European human rights standards also apply to the islands.

Åland was involved in its own right in the negotiations surrounding Finland's entry into the European Union. Contrary to the League of Nations situation in 1921, however, representatives of Åland participated in the negotiations as part of the Finnish delegation, as provided for in the Autonomy Act.

After two referenda in Åland and the consent of the Legislative Assembly, the Finnish government declared that the EC Treaty, the ecsc Treaty and the Euratom Treaty were applicable to the Åland Islands in accordance with the provisions set out in Protocol 2 of the Act concerning the Accession of Austria, Finland and Sweden to the European Union. This has been the case since 1.1.1995.

As an EU member, Finland is responsible for the implementation of EU law in Åland, even if it does not have any formal solutions for any lack of implementation or inaccurate implementation due to the principal of division of legislative powers between Finland and Åland under the Autonomy Act. This has increased the amount of interaction between the Finnish government and its counterpart in Åland, as was demonstrated during Finland's presidency of the EU in the second half of 2006.

Gunnar Jansson – Member of parliament from Åland 1983–2003

13 SÁMI PEOPLE

The Sámi people, whom other nations have referred to as Lapps or Laplanders, have inhabited the territory of present-day Finland since ancient times. Sámi ethnicity is based, above all, on language and culture; to be a Sámi is to be a member of a cultural group. Like other groups, Sámi people cannot be defined on grounds of race; they are an indigenous people, not just a language or an ethnic minority.

As an indigenous people, the Sámi have the constitutional right to cultural self-government, and this has been exercised by the Sámi Parliament, which was founded in 1996, and its predecessor, which was founded in 1973. Its 21 representatives are elected every four years in elections in the municipalities within the Sámi Domicile Area. The Sámi Parliament is responsible for defending the Sámi people's rights and monitoring matters related to their standing. It formulates proposals and initiatives and issues statements on matters within its jurisdiction, and also decides on the distribution of funds that have been granted to the Sámi people. The definition of an indigenous people is based on international law: they have a strong, living, historically unbroken association with a given region, and they have maintained their distinct cultural and social institutions, e.g. the village meetings of the Skolt Sámi. Indigenous peoples' rights are communal rights that apply to the whole group, whereas minority rights generally apply only to individuals. One of indigenous people's fundamental rights is their right to selfdetermination. Although this is recognised in the Finnish Constitution, it would appear that Finns have failed to really grasp the concept of the Sámi as an indigenous people.

There are almost 100,000 Sámi people, spread out over four countries. More than half of them live in Norway and the rest are in Sweden, Finland and Russia. Each country has a different definition of the Sámi people, so demographic statistics do not provide clear data on the exact numbers. Half of the Sámi people in Finland live in the Sámi Domicile Area in the northern municipalities of Inari, Enontekiö, Utsjoki and Sodankylä.

There are around ten Sámi languages, of which three – Northern, Skolt and Inari Sámi – are spoken in Finland. The most important Sámi municipality, Inari, is in practise a quatrilingual region. Around 70% of Finnish Sámi speak Northern Sámi, which is also used in Sweden and Norway. There are considerable differences between the Sámi languages, so speakers of different tongues cannot easily understand each other. The vast majority of Sámi people are illiterate in their mother tongue, since until recently all Sámi people received their basic education in the dominant Finnish language. This is despite the fact that the Sámi standard language was created around 400 years ago, only a few decades later than the Finnish standard language.

The status of the Sámi language in Finland is theoretically guaranteed by the Language Act, which states that Sámi people in the Sámi Domicile Area have the right to use their own language in official situations. In practice, however, the authorities are not generally required to speak Sámi, and interpreting services are needed.

Reindeer breeding, hunting and fishing are traditional sources of livelihood for the Sámi people, who have always been opposed to the excessive exploitation of natural resources. The Sámi culture is based on what the environment provides rather than intensive exploitation, construction or clearances. Reindeer, as arctic lichen-eating ruminants, are a good example of animals that are useful to people. They need only small amounts of water and are thus well adapted to the northern snow and ice-covered regions close to the tree line. Intensive forestry, clear-cutting and alterations to the surface environment destroy valuable lichen pastures and make it necessary to provide the reindeer with supplementary feeding, which can make it too expensive to practice this livelihood.

The Sámi culture is currently fragmented, and an intensive assimilation process is under way. Finnish philosopher Olli Lagerspetz has said that contented natives indicate that the dominant culture has been successful in its colonisation, whereas protesting natives indicate that colonisation and assimilation has not yet succeeded, and must therefore be continued. In the Finnish context, Sámi reindeer herders are the only voices raised against the destruction of forest pastures, but they have been able to defend their core cultural values.

It appears that the Finnish State still aims to assimilate the Sámi people into the dominant population – at least as far as their status as an indigenous people and their consequent rights are concerned. To prevent this process of assimilation and emigration, the Sámi Parliament has planned the creation of a cultural centre to promote the integration of the modern way of life into the traditional culture in a manner that would conserve strong basic values. The northern universities are already committed to cooperation through lectures and research. The Finnish government has understood the great importance of the cultural centre to halting the assimilation process, and that is probably why it has been in no hurry to provide funding for its construction.

But after all, the Sámi people only want to forge a civil society based on their own cultural heritage.

Pekka Aikio – Chair of the Sámi Parliament 1996–2008

SOCIAL POLICY

14 SOCIAL HOUSING

After the Second World War there was a considerable shortage of housing in Finland, which was intensified by migration from the countryside to towns that was brought about by structural changes in society. At the same time, the commercial banks had a limited possibility to grant loans, so social housing, the so-called Arava housing system, was established in 1949 in order to solve the problem.

Since the commercial banks were reluctant to issue secondary loans with higher risks, the Arava system adopted the granting of such loans as its core function.

In the 1950s and '60s the system granted loans for owner-occupied dwellings which promoted their construction. In addition to its housing policy objectives, the system strived to encourage citizens to save in advance for housing. This was considered an important way of ensuring ongoing economic development and reinforcing the banking system.

The basic idea was to provide public loans at reasonable rates of interest in order to guarantee that, having been granted an initial loan from a monetary institution, the buyer's own contribution would not become unreasonably high. The social impact of the idea was that the system allowed middle-class and even low-income workers to buy a place to live, and the proportion of owner-occupied dwellings rose relatively fast to over 70% of all dwellings. The system has offered hundreds of thousands of Finns a chance to get on the property ladder. Along with the educational system (innovations nos. 52 and 53), it has been one of the most important pillars of Finnish governmental policy, which aims for an egalitarian social structure.

The Arava system was not only restricted to granting reasonable public loans – it also had an impact on the quality and cost of construction as it took special notice of architectural quality and the functionality of new neighbourhoods. This means that it can still be claimed that many of the best housing areas in Finland are mainly constructed through Arava funding.

The idea was to build the new neighbourhoods so that they had a versatile social structure from the very beginning (innovation no. 15). The planning principle was that every housing area should include both non-subsidised and subsidised construction, and the distribution of building types should be diverse. Housing blocks were built relatively low, almost without exception with three or four storeys.

In the 1950s and '60s Arava housing consisted mainly of owner-occupied flats. As a result of rapid structural changes in the Finnish economy in the 1970s, the focus was shifted to the construction of rental accommodation. However, even then the areas were designed so that they would include both rental and owner-occupied flats.

Special attention was paid not only to quality but also to keeping the construction costs as reasonable as possible. Since the 1970s, construction firms were systematically asked to submit competitive offers.

Considering that Arava dwellings had a better price-quality relation and cheaper financing than other flats in the market, it was important to extend the benefits to cover more than just original buyers; those moving in later should also be able to benefit from the reasonable prices. It was thus ruled that owner-occupied Arava dwellings could only be sold to the municipality or to a buyer named by the municipality, and only at a regulated price that accounted for inflation but not other increases in value.

This practise also eliminated all forms of illegal pricing, which is always possible when the seller can choose the buyer. This solution enabled the municipality to offer not only rental dwellings but also reasonably priced owner-occupied flats for e.g. young first-time buyers, who are otherwise often at a disadvantage. The selling of rental dwellings is also regulated, which guarantees that the housing stock fulfils its original intention, especially in growing cities where there is a constant demand for reasonably priced rental dwellings.

Since the 1970s the Arava system supported in increasing amounts major repairs in building stock, and attention has also been paid to the buildings' energy-saving levels. All Arava dwellings have been constructed with at least tripleglazed windows since 1973, long before nonsubsidised housing.

When the Finnish monetary policy was loosening after the end of 1980s, considerable reforms were made to the Arava system. The most essential of these included the founding of the Housing Fund of Finland as a revolving fund. In the fund-model the incoming interest and amortization payments can be used as a revenue of the fund. The Fund can also acquire part of its necessary funding from the general financial and capital market.

An important development was that granting of interest subsidy loans displaced the direct lending of the Fund. In the interest subsidy-model the fund issues interest subsidies for commercial loans granted to developers. In order to obtain favourable interest level of these loans bidding process is used.

Between 1949 and 2005, Arava loans have financed the construction of approximately 950,000 dwellings and the basic renovation of approximately 250,000 dwellings. Approximately half of all constructed Arava dwellings were owner-occupied dwellings, while the other half were rental dwellings. Out of all dwellings, approximately 17% are Arava rental dwellings. Over 60% of rental dwellings are directly or indirectly owned by municipalities, while the vast majority of the rest are owned by non-profit organisations. Part of these organisations specialise in improving housing conditions for the elderly, students or other people living in poor conditions. These activities have an ever-increasing importance.

Martti Lujanen – Emeritus Deputy director general at the Ministry of the Environment

15 NO SLUMS

Helsinki was founded in 1550 but, having experienced several large fires, it has only been truly constructed after 1809. With the exception of old manors, no neighbourhoods in Helsinki were built exclusively for wealthy people. In the districts of e.g. Kruunuhaka and Ullanlinna, apart from the more expensive houses, there were always small rented flats too, although these would face towards the yard.

International guests often ask where Helsinki's slums are, and they become rather suspicious when they hear the answer: there are no slums in Finland.

This lack of slums can be explained by factors related to general economic development including: small income disparities compared to other countries, a highly developed Nordic welfare state, and a relatively small proportion of immigrants. The City of Helsinki's housing policy has also had a strong impact on this development.

First of all, Finnish municipalities have more extensive self-governance, including the power to raise taxes, than their counterparts in any other European country (innovation no. 4). Secondly, due to both historical reasons and intentional policies, the City of Helsinki is an important landowner within its borders, possessing approximately 70% of its territory. Town planning in

Finland has also been left entirely in the hands of the municipalities. The City of Helsinki can thus implement a fairly strong housing policy if it so desires.

During the last 50 years the City of Helsinki has practised an intensive social housing policy, even to the extent that, especially in recent years, neighbouring localities have seen a jump in their tax revenue.

Almost without exception, new housing areas are planned according to the concept that there must be accommodation to suit all social classes. Rich and the poor live side by side, and social housing (innovation no. 14) is no different in quality or appearance from so-called hard money housing.

The City of Helsinki's housing policy has naturally been influenced by state subsidies and directives. Helsinki was a wealthy city for a long time and state subsidies for housing were considerable, but the State's contribution has gradually declined since the early 1990s. At the same time, the State has substantially cut the city's share of corporate tax revenues. The municipalities are thus obliged to compete with each other for "good taxpayers".

It remains to be seen whether the social housing policy implemented in Helsinki can withstand external attacks.

The principle of social mixing can be considered a significant social innovation. Inequality related to dwelling place and housing conditions can easily give rise to hereditary marginalisation and disadvantages, but we have been able to prevent this unfavourable development in Helsinki, at least for the time being.

Pekka Korpinen – Deputy Mayor of Helsinki 1991–2007

16 Y-FOUNDATION

A normal life and social empowerment requires decent housing and a safe environment. A home is a place of one's own that means much more than just security: it is the key to a socially acceptable life. Once they are provided with a home and appropriate support, most homeless people are able to cope on their own; rehabilitation and supported housing enable the homeless to live independent lives.

Good supported housing allows the investment that has been made in the social and health services to deliver results. Supported housing for young people is a lifelong investment, and the provision of decent housing is essential to the stability and cohesion of society.

Tackling homelessness is not cheap, but the long-term costs of ignoring it are much higher in terms of economic expenditure, social problems and criminality – no matter how they are measured. Finding permanent solutions to homelessness requires a range of actions: housing, social and health services, support services and the management of social housing.

The Y-Foundation, which was founded in 1985 to supply homes for the homeless and refugees, is one practical means of tackling homelessness in Finland. The founding members of the foundation are The Finnish Association for Mental Health, The Finnish Red Cross, the National Ecclesiastical Board, the Confederation of Finnish Construction Industries, the Construction Union, the Association of Finnish Local Authorities, and the cities of Helsinki, Espoo, Vantaa, Tampere and Turku (the five largest cities in Finland). The Y-Foundation buys one-room flats and commissions the building of new homes for rent. The flats are situated among the normal housing stock to avoid social segregation and the creation of slums, and this model is also followed in the building of new blocks.

One key objective is to offer normal, permanent housing – not temporary shelters or dormitories. Everyone has a right to a decent life.

The provision of housing is funded mainly by loans from the state and credit institutions, grants from Alko and Finland's Slot Machine Association (innovation no. 70) and of course the Y-Foundation itself, which cooperates with local authorities, parishes and various NGO's to arrange support and services for tenants.

Using local networks means that the authorities' and voluntary organisations' potential can be fully realised. Rehabilitation services and support can be coordinated to help the homeless, and this support compliments the housing facilities to create viable long-term housing solutions.

In 1986 there were almost 20,000 homeless people in Finland, but the number today is significantly lower (about 8,000). In 2005 Y-Foundation owned over 6,300 apartments in 49 municipalities across Finland.

Y-Foundation is also involved in international networks – it is affiliated to e.g. the United Nations Human Settlements Programme unhabitat, and is a member of FEANTSA, the European Federation of National Organisations working with the Homeless.

Hannu Puttonen – General manager,
Y-Foundation 1996–2012

17 STUDENT ACCOMMODATION

According to the latest research and current demand Finland has sufficient student housing (apart from the Helsinki areas), which means that a major obstacle to social mobility has been removed – everybody can now apply to study knowing that there will be reasonably priced student accommodation near the school or university.

Student housing organisations were mostly founded in the late 1960s and the beginning of the 1970s, after the state began granting loans for student house construction in 1966. Student organisations and municipalities created foundations or municipally owned organisations, which always include student, tenant and town representatives on their boards.

The way that the student housing issue was handled is a typical example of how Finns solve problems: despite a lack of resources the first houses were built in several towns over 30 years ago and, with the help of state loans, continued to rise one by one on building sites that municipalities had reserved for this purpose. 30 years later construction is complete, loans are being paid off, older houses have even been renovated, and the student housing problem has been solved.

When student housing organisations were founded, they sat down together with student unions and drew up some basic principles. Most of these still apply, and there are some interesting differences compared to other European countries.

Each town has only one student housing organisation, which takes care of all the student housing in that area. Student accommodation is nothing to do with universities or colleges.

Student housing organisations are independent of schools. This means that, unlike many other European countries where student accommodation in is reserved for university students only, Finnish student housing is available to any student, irrespective of what they choose to study after high school. It is also rather common in Finland for student families to occupy student flats.

Student accommodation is situated away from the campus areas (with some famous exceptions), and the houses are not dormitories but regular blocks of flats. The most common type of student accommodation is a two or three bedroom flat, in which students have their own room and a shared kitchen and bathroom. This type of flat can also be easily altered for family use. New student accommodation is comprised of studio flats for single students and small family flats.

The goal of reasonably priced and safe accommodation near the school for every student who needs it has basically been accomplished. Student housing organisations have also been able to contribute to the internationalisation strategies of local schools and universities: Finland is, rather surprisingly, one of the most popular student exchange countries in Europe. This is because of the English-language programmes that schools offer, but credit can also be claimed by the local student housing organisation, which arranges visitors' accommodation.

Ulla-Mari Karhu – Managing director,
Finland's student housing LTD 2000–2008

18 24-HOUR SERVICE HOMES

At over a hundred events I have asked the audience to tell me the largest group of people in Finland that live in 24-hour service homes, meaning a decent flat (with at least a toilet, running water, kitchenette and living room) with 24-hour service or surveillance. People usually suggest the elderly, or sometimes even prisoners in their cells, but nobody has yet come up with the right answer.

Which is of course: we family people. Every day there are phone calls asking what time you will be home, saying there's nothing to eat in the fridge, telling you to buy cat food, wondering who you are drinking with, and suggesting that you don't drink quite as much as you did the night before. There is strict control, but when homemade bread and a full breakfast sits waiting for you in the morning you have to admit that the service is excellent. But what about those who live alone, people with no family? Does anyone care?

In the 1980s, Finland, which was at that time the most institutionalised country in the world, started to move towards a more out-patient based system. As the elderly population grew in relative terms and became more frail, so began the construction of homes for the aged, followed by nursing homes and then whole buildings for the elderly. The amount of services provided was increased gradually, first focusing on daylight hours and then being implemented on a 24-hour basis.

But people under 65 were forgotten. When the capacity of mental hospitals was cut – the amount of beds was slashed from 20,000 to 6,000 – patients were decanted into dilapidated dormitories and nursing or rehabilitation homes, and the same was true of mentally handicapped people. Alcoholics were also packed off to shabby dorms and hostels, as were criminals released from prison.

When the sub-tenancy system was practically abolished by the construction of student flats (innovation no. 17) in the 1970s – 20 years later than it was in Sweden – the only big groups obliged to live in such conditions were the mentally ill, the mentally handicapped and a section of the senile elderly and neurologically disabled. Their numbers run into thousands.

According to the Services and Assistance for the Disabled Act (1988) the housing conditions of the severely disabled were to be sorted out by 1992, and this was successful with regards to physically disabled and visually or aurally impaired people, for whom their respective organisations built over a thousand independent one-room flats. The acts and regulations regarding the disabled were not applied to the mentally ill or mentally handicapped, however, so their housing conditions remained considerably poorer – as did their social status. People who become ill at an early age are left with only the state pension, but this was meant to provide security in old age, not for young people to live on.

There are three big groups that benefit from 24-hour service homes:

1. A section of people living alone: approximately 10% of mentally ill people that live alone cannot cope by themselves.
2. The service homes would allow a couple of thousand people who live in institutions to carry on a normal life at a decreased cost to the state.
3. There are approximately 70,000 adult Finns still living with their elderly parents or family members. This number includes e.g. government officials, students and single people who are taking care of their parents, but is mainly comprised of men (85%) and women (15%) who for one reason or another have failed to find their feet.

There is no comprehensive study on this group. Oiva Antti Mäki studied 3,500 mentally handicapped adults living with their parents for his doctoral theses, and the name of his publication says it all: I wish I could live a day longer than my child. Most of the people in this group would like to live more independently, in service homes, but they cannot cope by themselves and are not willing to live in group homes or institutions.

According to estimates, at least 2,000 service homes should be constructed for the mentally ill, and other 2,000 for the mentally handicapped – part of them for neurologically handicapped people, alcoholics and people released from prison. It is impossible to abolish homelessness without constructing 24-hour service homes. Their construction could be partly financed by the money that would be saved by removing people from institutions, but the problem is not the construction itself but the fact that decisions regarding 24-hour service home maintenance is decentralised, in the hands of almost 500 municipalities which have so far preferred to locate people in privately owned, generally substandard group homes ("service homes"). The basic requirement should be decent accommodation, and services could then be privately arranged to complement this.

Finland's Slot Machine Association (innovation no. 67), Y-Foundation (innovation no. 16), ASPA Housing Services Foundation, and certain other foundations including disabled people's organisations have now started to construct a network of 24-hour service homes in Finland, but only 25% of the needs of people under 65 have been met. The only way to remedy this situation is to work at a faster pace.

Ilkka Taipale – Member of parliament 1971–1975, 2000–2007

19 STATUS OF THE ROMANI POPULATION

The Romani people came to Finland in the late sixteenth century from Sweden and Russia. As was the case all over Europe, they were ill received. Their lifestyle, culture and language were considered alien. A law passed in 1637 made it legal to hang any Roma who resisted an expulsion order. In the seventeenth century, the Church began to improve the living conditions of the Roma and to keep records of the group. The clergy was encouraged to make the Roma socially acceptable through baptism. All homeless wanderers were locked up in workhouses, from which the Roma were later transferred to a penitentiary in Hämeenlinna on the basis of a law passed in 1863. Even in the year 1900, a committee handling the "Gypsy issue" considered the best policy to be the complete assimilation of the Romani people into the general populace. The main assimilation methods were children's education and registration. The Roma were seen as children who must be educated and monitored.

It was a long time before the government made any new forays into Romani policy. In 1953, the government set up a Gypsy Committee, whose task was to "examine the Gypsy issue, particularly the assimilation of Gypsies into normal social life, their employment and compulsory education". In 1956, the government tasked the Advisory Board on Gypsy Affairs (now the Advisory Board on Romani Affairs) with monitoring and following the development of the social circumstances of the Romani population, making the necessary improvement proposals. The Advisory Board is the main nationwide organisation looking after the welfare of the Roma in Finland. Radicals of the 1960s highlighted the failings in the living conditions of the underprivileged, trying to act as the voice of the discriminated, the poor, the sick and other minorities. Worth a particular mention is the November Movement (innovation no. 34). 1960s radicalism also led to the 1967 petitionary motion in Parliament for "the creation of a Committee to solve the problems of the Gypsies and the allocation of public funds for practical measures". This was the first motion that talked about looking after the "interests" of the Romani people and to clearly emphasise the "right of the minority" to participate in it. Thus the Roma were awarded their first representative in the Advisory Board.

The Romani issue had its most concrete aspect in the lack of housing, and in 1975 a temporary Special Housing Act was passed, including a special funding system. The aim was that by the end of 1980, the housing situation of the Roma would be the same as that of the population at large. The validity of the law was later extended by one year. The law is an example of a special statute giving a specific ethnic group privileges above the rest of the population – i.e. positive discrimination. Although the housing conditions of the Roma improved significantly, it became apparent that the special statute could not improve the circumstances of those who were worst off. Not all the targets set for the statute were met. Better ways of improving the housing conditions of the Roma include for example increasing the number of state-funded rented accommodation.

The reformed Advisory Board on Romani Affairs gave a report in principle on the position of the Roma. The report stated that Finnish society had always approached the Romani issue from the point of view of the majority and never from that of the distinct Romani culture. This significant change in approach was reflected in a 1992 report of the Finnish Fundamental Rights Committee, which stated that all citizens must have equal rights to legal protection, their own language and their own culture.

A fundamental rights reform was made to the Constitution Act in 1995. Of particular importance were the anti-discrimination clauses: "No one shall, without an acceptable reason, be treated differently from other persons on the ground of sex, age, origin, language, religion, conviction, opinion, health, disability or other reason that concerns his or her person." Origin refers to national, ethnic and social backgrounds. The term "origin" is considered also to include the concepts of race and skin colour.

The law (now the Finnish Constitution) states: "The Sámi, as an indigenous people, as well as the Roma and other groups, have the right to maintain and develop their own language and culture." The legislation therefore specifically mentions two traditional minorities of the Finnish population: the Sámi (innovation no. 13) and the Roma.

Mother tongue is an extremely important factor in identity-building. According to the Basic Education Act, students with Sámi, Romani or sign language, or some other foreign language as their mother tongue, have the right to receive instruction in their mother tongue for at least two hours per week. In 1996, the Research Institute for the Languages of Finland set up a Romani Language Committee tasked with developing, maintaining and researching the Romani language. The Child Day Care Act (innovation no. 23) now also includes as a target supporting the language and culture of Roma children in cooperation with representatives of the Romani culture. The same policy had been adopted in all educational legislation related to primary and secondary education, as well as senior secondary education for adults.

Today, Finland's Romani population has full civil rights and civic duties. Finland's Roma are considered by themselves and by others to be both Finns and Roma. Most Roma live in urban areas, and the majority has permanent housing. Their lives as vagrants are a thing of the past. Most Roma are registered as members of the Lutheran Church. Due to a lower level of education, Finland's Roma have a weaker financial and social status than the average Finn. The legislation may be equitable, but social attitudes have to a great extent retained their traditional mistrust. Not all doors are open to the Roma. The EU has expanded so much that poor Romani people from abroad, especially Romania, have appeared on the streets of Helsinki. There is discussion in Finland about whether they should be helped here or sent back to their homeland. Begging in Finland is rare, but is permitted.

Kyösti Suonoja – Assistant professor,
Romano missio chairman 2004–2006

20 HOUSING COMPANY MODEL

The manner in which apartment block ownership and administration can be effectively managed is an issue which has come to the forefront in the privatisation process of new EU member states. In these cases attention is given to ensuring the continuous maintenance and renovation of communal structures and facilities, such as the roof, walls, stairwells and lifts, and of utilities, such as water, sewage and electrical systems.

The issue has also been a topic of interest in several old EU member states, where the legislative solution for home ownership in apartment blocks is either non-existent or lacking in efficacy.

In most cases the legislative solution applied has been the "condominium model", which involves a specifically designated "home owners association" or the administration is organised based on a housing condominium-only solution.

The problem with the housing condominium-only solution is that the home owners comanage the maintenance and repair of communal structures and facilities without any specifically designated decision making body. It is clear that this kind of solution produces a number of administrative problems.

A much more effective solution is to combine the condominium model with "home owners associations". However, this model is also clearly lacking in several areas. These are especially difficulties in decision-making and obtaining loans for major repairs concerning common structures and facilities.

These problems were solved in Finland with a special ownership model for apartment buildings and terraced houses. In this model the buildings are owned by the housing company, and the shares are divided in such a way that they correspond to an ownership of a certain flat. Separate legislation was developed for this model.

The highest authority is exercised by the shareholders' meeting, which is usually held twice a year. Each shareholder can vote according to the number of shares he or she owns. The number of shares is generally based on the size of the flat.

The shareholders' meeting approves, among others, a budget, which is used to verify the monthly payments by shareholders. The shareholders' meeting also makes decisions concerning major property repairs. The shareholders' meeting also elects the board of directors, which exercises decision-making power. The board consists in general of at least three members.

The board appoints a superintendent (manager), who is responsible for, among other things, collecting monthly payments and keeping company accounts. The superintendent also prepares various repair-bid documents for the company board, even though the board makes all decisions concerning the selection of contractors for instance for major repairs.

Superintendents are usually employed by a property management agency. Such agencies are usually in charge of at least ten housing companies.

The share certificate of each apartment can be used as flexible collateral when taking out loans for purchasing property or making repairs to the apartment. Alternatively, the company can take out loans against mortgage collateral for making repairs to communal structures and facilities. This makes it possible to take out loans at the most favourable market rates.

Company-specific loan interest rates and instalments are paid in connection with the monthly payments. These monthly payments are sufficient enough to cover the costs for company administration, repairs and also heating. If the apartment owner fails to pay the monthly payments, the company can take possession of the apartment in question and pay the unpaid amount using revenue earned from rent. In cases such as this, however, the owner does not lose his/her ownership.

The following are some of the benefits offered by a liability housing company:
1. Decision-making responsibilities are clearly defined and the property's communal structures and facilities have one specified owner.
2. Loans can be granted, on one hand, for repairs of communal structures and facilities and, on the other, apartment-specific needs (the purchase of the flat and apartment-specific repairs).
3. To sell housing company shares referring to a certain flat is easy for the owner to do (e.g. easier than selling a car).

4. The sanctioning system for those who have not paid their maintenance charge is functioning well, which means that these sanctions are rarely used.
5. The result of this clearly-defined decisionmaking process is that the buildings and their communal structures and facilities are in good condition and adequate repair measures can be taken. This is crucial to ensuring that property value is maintained and the living standard is kept high.
6. Shareholders can be either individual people or companies, municipalities or non-profit organisations. Individual people can either live in their own dwelling or rent it out. As a result, the housing company model enables the integration of owner-occupied dwellings and rental dwellings in the same buildings and thus decreases segregation.

The Housing Company system has been functioning in Finland without any greater problems already from 1920. As a consequence of this the share of Housing Company dwellings in the housing stock is as high as 45%.

In conclusion, the Finnish Housing Company model provides a clear and transparent ownership structure which is easy to understand by every one.

Martti Lujanen – Emeritus Deputy Director general at the Ministry of the Environment

21 EMPLOYMENT PENSION SCHEME

The need for an employment pension scheme is not a Finnish invention: in all developed economies, the livelihood of the majority is based on paid work, and when paid work finishes due to old age or loss of working ability, it is replaced by an employment pension. Therefore an earnings-related pension acts as insurance against the termination of earnings.

Neither are the basic solutions used in pension systems (defined benefit plans vs. defined contribution plans) nor the funding alternatives (pay-as-you-go or pre-funded), or even the idea that there are useful intermediate forms of these alternatives, Finnish inventions.

Nor was Finland the first to come up with the intricate pattern for interaction between employment pensions and the labour market. Many other countries have made the same choices as Finland, starting by realising the usefulness of early retirement pensions in removing the elderly from the way of young people's employment opportunities, and leading to recognising the complex behaviour models and attitudes that these mechanisms bring about.

What can be considered a Finnish invention is the way in which the country's many choices regarding the employment pension scheme have been compiled into a single well-functioning entity. Another Finnish creation is the decisionmaking process with which this entity can be adjusted to adapt to the social situation of the times, while maintaining the basic concept of the system and ensuring that the changes treat all groups equally.

Earnings-related pensions are meant to replace earnings. This leads to a defined benefit system and a target level of approximately sixty per cent. The same cover must be available to all citizens, so the system is regulated by law and all-encompassing. Thanks to the pension system being set in law it has been easy to ensure that people can retain the pensions they have earned even when changing jobs. Thus the pension system supports the free movement of workers, which is one of the Four Freedoms of the European Union.

If employment pensions are not linked to an index that is at least equivalent to consumer prices, they cannot fulfil their task when there is inflation. Therefore an index guarantee equivalent or superior to inflation is needed. Inflation is not an insurable risk, so the cost of the index link is covered jointly with a pay-as-you-go system. This makes it possible to guarantee.

Partial, though significant, pre-funding helps to even out premium level differences between generations. It has led to funds equivalent to a large proportion of the national economy (100 billion euros, i.e. two thirds of the gross domestic product). Thanks to pre-funding, the premium percentage rises much more slowly than the pension expenditure rate.

Administration of the pension system is shared between pension insurance companies, pension trusts and pension funds. Benefits are the same regardless of the pension company, so a procedure is needed by which unfunded benefits and the premiums collected for them are pooled between all pension institutions. The pool has from the start been regulated by a well-functioning clearing and cost allocation procedure.

The decentralised organisation also allows for a certain amount of competition. In relation to statutory pensions regulated by law, there cannot be as much competition as in normal business; however, the decentralised implementation allows for more competition in terms of investment activities, service quality and efficiency than statutory pension systems generally allow. The decentralised system also means that this major portion of the national economy is not exposed to dangerously high risk.

For the policy owner, decentralisation does not mean increased complexity: this has been ensured with the "last-instance principle", which means that the policy holder only needs to deal with one pension institution.

Our employment pension scheme represents Finnish social innovation at its best: it is a balanced system made up of diverse elements and developed with joint effort in order to respond to the needs of society at each time.

Kari Puro – CEO, Ilmarinen mutual pension insurance company 1991–2006

22 CHILD DAY CARE

After the Second World War, Finland was a poor and war-stricken country. Women participated in the labour market partly in order to compensate for the missing male labour force, partly because of the country's long history of gender equality. After the war, they stayed in paid employment. In the 1960s, the country that previously had relied on small-scale farming became urbanised faster than any other country in Europe: young people headed for cities to find jobs and to study. This further increased the need for women in the labour market, as well as their labour market participation. Child day care, however, was in short supply.

In 1973, a Child Day Care Act entered into force in Finland that obliged local authorities to provide day care, with central government subsidising the activities financially. A heated debate on the "institutionalisation of children" had taken place at the time of drafting the Act: right-wingers opposed the Act, underlining the importance of children being cared for at home by their mothers, while left-wingers were for the Act, using the existing labour market situation as their justification. The Act gave rise to a social innovation: the creation of the occupation of family child-minder. Family child-minders' work consisted of caring for a group of 5 children, including their own children. They were paid a salary (by the parents and the local authority), and the work generated pension rights and called for a special education.

On entering the 1980s, the development of day care was too slow to meet the need. Parental leave had been extended to nine months. The Centre Party, the former agrarian party, then developed home care allowance – a social innovation (no. 23) – which was paid to the parents if one of them stayed at home to care for their children under school age. The political left-wing opposed, suspecting that the reform would set a trap for women: they would exit the labour market and get into a disadvantaged labour market position, as well as lose part of their pensions. In 1984, a political compromise was reached that again gave rise to a social innovation: legislation on support to child day care, which took effect gradually up to 1990.

The legislation on child day care gave the parents the right to decide on their child's day care after parental leave (11 months at that time): they could choose between day care provided by the local authorities (at a day-care centre or in family day care) and home care allowance that they could use according to their own judgement. The right only applied to families with children under three. The child day-care legislation aimed to ensure a secure life for the youngest children in particular. The implication for the local authorities was that their obligation to provide child day care was dramatically increased. However, with the help of central government transfers, the local authorities managed to fulfil their obligations.

Home care allowance was distributed to the carers of 11,000 children in 2000. Since then, women's participation in the labour market has become more common and there has been a corresponding rise in the number of children in municipal daycare. The number of children receiving home care allowance in 2010 was 98,000.

The current figure for children under three years old is 383 euros per month, and a smaller sum is paid for children under six.

Opinions have been voiced in public, according to which women's careers are harmed by the years they spend looking after children at home, and municipal daycare is recommended to remedy this. Municipal daycare institutions in Finland are nowadays "full". However, it is vital that the home care allowance survives. The personal circumstances of families with children and mothers vary, as do the guiding principles of childcare and raising children. The home care allowance gives many women in Finland the economic opportunity to care for their offspring at home during their most sensitive years. According to social psychologists children are then "ready" for group activities with their peers when they turn three.

In this respect Finland is different from the other Nordic countries: In Denmark, Sweden and Norway over 90% or children under three are cared for in daycare centres, but in Finland the figure is 67%.

Only 40% of children under two are in daycares in Finland, but the figures for Norway, Sweden and Denmark are 60%, 70% and 88% respectively.

Vappu Taipale – Minister for Health and Social Affairs 1982–1984, Director General, Stakes (National RND Centre for social welfare and health) 1992–2008

22 CHILD HOME-CARE ALLOWANCE

The child home-care allowance is a family policy subsidy for people who take care of their under 3-year-old at home, and therefore do not exercise their right to use a municipal daycare. I suggested a subsidy system for child home-care already in the late 1950s, but it took three decades to become reality.

It all started when I had finished my studies and had also participated in working life and wanted to stay at home with our three small children. I was encouraged by the opinion of child psychologist, who said that to secure favourable development, a child's two, and preferably three, first years should be spent in the care of one and the same person. Different day-care carers have different characteristics, and this restlessness was considered undesirable for babies and toddlers. It was not as easy in the 1950s to hire nannies as it had been in earlier times but, on the other hand, the proportion of women in our labour force rose to 40% while it was only 26% in Sweden.

However, the reality was that when a mother stayed at home to take care of her children, family income diminished and consumption declined; if the children were in municipal day-care the mother could continue in paid work. The family paid for day-care according to its ability, but the payment only covered part of the real costs, as working mothers also gathered a pension while those at home lost out. In my opinion, young families who performed this valuable task were placed in an unfair situation.

As I was a journalist, I started writing articles on this social injustice, and even took the issue to the Association of Population Policy's board of directors, who took an interest because the Finnish birth rate was declining alarmingly. I also raised the question with the Centre Party (at that time Agrarian Party), which included the child home-care allowance, or mother's salary as it was first called, in its agenda in 1962. We founded a working group on family policy and constructed a legislative proposal on the issue.

I also acquainted myself with the Soviet day-care system, which was created after the Revolution. All mothers of small children were in paid work in order to contribute to the construction of society and the system. Children were in public day-care centres. In contrast, we who supported the child home-care allowance were of the opinion that families in a democracy should be able to exercise freedom of choice with regards to child care, and that this should also be financially supported by society. The corresponding State committee supported the proposal, but its opposing counterpart objected to it in government negotiations. When the Centre Party formed a minority government (innovation no. 7) in 1976, a pilot child homecare allowance scheme was launched.

One would have assumed that this reform would gain easy approval, but that was not the case. The most significant adversary was the Social Democratic Party, which wanted the subsidy to be directed specifically at mothers who were already in working life. They claimed that the Centre Party was pushing a subsidy for farm owners who were at home in any case, even though the reality was that only a couple of thousand of the 60,000 children born each year were born to farmers. The academic women's associations also opposed the child home-care allowance on the grounds that they felt it would hinder women's career development.

The issue was disputed for several years, especially between the two major parties, both among mps and within the government. I even personally clashed with my colleague, Minister Vappu Taipale. In 1986 the child home-care allowance was finally approved, to be granted for children under age three, after the parental allowance period, and it was also paid for other children under school age. In 1990 all children under the age of three were entitled to the subjective right to day-care (innovation no. 22), which was pushed by the Social Democratic Party. That settled the political disagreement over the matter. According to child psychologists, children over the age three would have had a particular need for day-care to aid their development, but it was a good start.

Child home-care allowance was at its height at the beginning of the 1990s, when it was granted to 150,000 families, but the ensuing years of economic depression cut this number by 20%, and it still has not risen back to its initial level; in 2004 it was granted to 138,000 families in Finland. The allowance is 294 euros per month for the first child under three years of age, 84 euros for any other child under three, and 50 euros for any other child under school age. The system covers 60% of children under two years of age and approximately 30% of children under six.

There are interesting differences in the proportion of children in home-care and day-care centres in Finland and other Nordic countries, where there is no child home-care allowance. More than 50% of two-year-olds in Finland are cared for at home, while in Denmark and Sweden the proportion is only 13%.

Marjatta Väänänen – Minister for social affairs 1982–1983

24 PATERNITY LEAVE

A couple of years ago British women's organisations ran a campaign titled "I'd rather be a mother in Finland" but there could just as easily have been a parallel campaign called "I'd rather be a father in Finland" for men.

The Nordic countries are way ahead of the rest of the EU pack with regards to parenthood, and especially fatherhood, benefits fathers rarely have the right to independent paternity leave or allowances outwith this geographical area.

The importance of the father's role as an active parent started to be emphasised in the 1970s, until which time he had been considered as little more than a provider of sperm and financial support.

Throughout the 1980s, however, men were encouraged to visit Maternity and Well-baby Clinics (innovation no. 39) with their pregnant partners and participate in the childbearing process.

In Finland the right to paternity leave was introduced in 1978 after a decade-long debate which also involved the development of a new gender ideology. In 1985 maternity allowance was changed to parental allowance, which could, with the mother's agreement, be partly used by the father, and in the 1990s the whole system was reformed to encourage more fathers to make use of it. The right to 6 days' paid leave, which was introduced at the beginning of 1991, was targetted directly at fathers. In the severe depression of 1993 the total period of parental allowance was shortened, but post partum paternity leave no longer decreased the parental allowance. Since 1997 it has also been possible to postpone this paternity leave rather than take it directly after the birth.

Finnish parental allowance is now paid for 263 working days; the first 105 days (maternity leave) is paid to the mother (maternity allowance), while the following 158 days (parental leave) can be paid to either the mother or father (parental allowance).

Fathers are also entitled to up to 18 working days leave (paternity leave), which can be taken at any time during maternity or parental leave. Paternity leave can be split into a maximum of four periods, and if this includes the last 12 days of parental leave the father is entitled to an extended paternity leave of 24 working days after the parental leave has expired. This is called the father's month.

Since the 1990s the level of parental leave taken has remained stable, with paternity leave being taken by approximately two thirds of entitled men. This figure is still growing as the possibilities to take fatherhood leave were extended in 2010. Around 20–35% of fathers take the full month off. Paternity leave is taken more frequently by middle-income white-collar workers and specialists in the social, health care and education sector, but it is also used by those in the technical sector and industry. Compared with public sector employees, those in the private sector take shorter paternity leave, and the full paternity leave is most frequently claimed by men from the social and health care sector and agricultural workers.

A study revealed that the main reasons that fathers might not use the full leave they are entitled to were the insufficiency of the allowance to compensate for lost income and the harmful effect that it might have on their careers or ongoing tasks in the workplace. These reasons were offered by fathers themselves.

I myself had the pleasure of taking paternity leave twice from my post of Minister of Justice in Paavo Lipponen's government (Lipponen was also on paternity leave from his Prime Minister's post). I took one-week paternity leave immediately after the births of both of my daughters and combined the remaining days with my summer holiday. I do not think that this did me any harm, but rather had a positive impact on bringing about a more equal parenthood.

Johannes Koskinen – Minister of justice 1999–2005, chairman on constitutional committee 2011–

25 MATERNITY PACK

The Finnish maternity pack was an important social innovation when it was introduced, and it is still unique in the world in terms of both scope and content. Although mothers in other countries have also been entitled to various grants which have included child care items, these have mainly consisted of individual pieces of clothing. Part of the reason that the maternity grant came to consist of a pack of child care items was the short supply of goods in post-war Finland – rationing meant that here were things that money just could not buy. The maternity pack was "The State's Present to Finnish Mothers" at that time, and it really met a need.

In the beginning the municipality's social welfare board decided what type of maternity grant each claimant was entitled to. There were three different types of packs; one with products for both mother and child, one with only child care items (such as a 'navel girdle' and swaddling clothes), and one with only products for the mother (such as sheeting, towels and sewing materials).

Entitlement to the maternity grant was extended to all mothers in 1949 irrespective of their financial status, the only exception being mothers in institutions or prisons who were not entitled until 1977.

The clothes were initially all made of traditional fabrics, with the more frills the better, and underpants and romper suits were added to in the 1950s when they became part of contemporary babywear. Novelties in the 1960s included a bonnet, a sleeping bag and disposable nappies, and in the '70s traditional fabrics were replaced by colourful stretch-terry romper suits and clothes. Up until this time garments had been made of white or unbleached cotton, which mothers would decorate and embroider themselves. The pack was completed in the 1980s with several new items such as socks, a thermal blanket with a zip, and a sleeping bag/pram suit. Until this time the emphasis had been on the high quality of the clothes, but now more attention was paid to the overall colour scheme as well. The last ten years have seen plenty of new additions in keeping with current fashions, and cotton sweatshirts, daysuits, reusable nappies, bodies, tights and quilted suits are all now included.

In addition to clothes, the pack has always contained other child care items too. The thing that people tend to remember best is an enamel basin that was used for washing the baby or the baby's clothes – or both – before bathrooms and washing machines became common. The basin dropped out of the pack in the 1970s. Fathers have been taken more and more into account in the selection of the contents, as well as in the enclosed information leaflets, and there have been plans to change the term "maternity pack". The pack handbook that used to be called "To Mother" had its name changed to "We're Having a Baby" in the 1980s for the same reason.

In the 1980s, when the pack was under the jurisdiction of the former National Board of Social Welfare, attention began to be paid not only to the overall quality of the pack but also to the promotion of the child's mental development. "Our Baby's Book" had to be specifically made for the maternity pack because this kind of picture book had yet to become commercially available. The pack was also completed with a toy for a newborn: a rattle made of yellow fabric with a smiling face on one side and a grumpy face on the other. Both the book and the rattle have become hits with the babies.

The maternity pack has marked a turning point in Finnish society. A precondition for receiving the pack is that the mother should visit a prenatal clinic before the fourth month of pregnancy, so practically all pregnant women register with the health care services. Maternal and infant mortality rates have decreased in Finland since the 1950s so dramatically that the country has long been among the top three countries in the world. This might not have been possible without the attraction of the maternity pack.

Sirpa Taskinen – Emerita Development manager, Stakes

26 FREE SCHOOL MEALS

Students in Finland in comprehensive schools (innovation no. 52), high schools and vocational institutions (innovation no. 53) are provided with a free daily meal on schooldays. School catering has a long history, having been officially regulated for almost a hundred years, and in the 21st century it still plays a fundamental part in student welfare.

In Finland the importance of school meals to an improved learning capacity was understood as early as the 17th century, when schoolboys received food and other items as aid as they went around the countryside. School kitchens were considered necessary to promote Latin language studies. School meals were discussed for the first time in the Elementary School Convention of 1896, and the state started to subsidise them in 1913.

Preparations for new legislation started in the 1930s when the National Board of General Education published a book on primary school children's nutrition, which declared that there was no doubt about the necessity of school meals.

In 1943 Finland was the first country in the world to enact a law on free school meals for all pupils, who were obliged to do a reasonable amount of work outside school hours to grow and collect food for the school kitchen. The goal of providing every pupil in compulsory education with a free school meal on every school day within five years was realised in 1948, and the system has endured to this day.

Regulations pertaining to education have since been reformed and specified, which has meant more guidance on practical school meal arrangements. At present the free school meal is eaten by approximately 900,000 children and young people on a daily basis.

The school catering system guarantees students a free and balanced warm meal on every school day, providing for student health and at the same time the well-being of the whole school community. School catering and monitoring the health of pupils on special diet are a natural part of student welfare work.

The Finnish school meal is versatile and balanced, and the catering is designed to promote the health, growth and development of pupils with regards to their age and condition. School meals cover part of children's and young people's daily nutritional requirements and complement other meals consumed during the day. Attention is paid to the provision of a healthy, versatile and attractive dish with optional ingredients. Apart from providing an enjoyable meal, attention is also paid to a clean and pleasant dining environment, and peaceful, unhurried dining. Pupils can participate in the catering system by e.g. helping and guiding younger pupils or by doing their work experience placement in the school kitchen. Pupils' participation in the practical arrangements contributes to their appreciation of the meal and the promotion of joint responsibility.

School catering is also an elemental part of Finnish food culture. School meals generally consist of basic Finnish food; a good meal includes a warm dish, a salad, grated vegetables or a piece of fresh fruit or vegetable, bread, margarine and a drink. National, local and seasonal variations are taken into account in the menu, which is developed together with pupils and staff as well as parents. Theme days are organised to break the routine, traditional festival meals are served where applicable, and international food and customs are explored.

The school meal is designed to complement the rhythm of the school day, and the current debate is leaning towards offering the pupil a nutritious and balanced snack in a pleasant environment in accordance with their schedule. The options are a free or paid school snack or a packed snack from home. Pupils who participate in morning or afternoon activities are always served a snack.

School meals are also an integral part of pupils' education and upbringing, which is the joint responsibility of schools and families. They have a key role in this process because eating habits learned at an early age can have life-long health effects. In the 21st century there has been a growing concern over increasing levels of obesity among schoolchildren, and school education is seen as vital weapon in curbing this trend. The daily rhythm, food and exercise should be balanced in such a way as to promote both learning and well-being at school, and support the integral structure of children's working days. A free warm school meal is thus one of our secrets for engendering successful learning (innovation no. 54), know-how and well-being.

Kirsi Lindroos – General director, Finnish national board of education 2003–2007

27 CARING FOR DISABLED WAR VETERANS

After World War II there were nearly 100,000 permanently disabled war veterans in a country of 4 million inhabitants. Altogether more than 200,000 Finns were wounded during the war. Ongoing compensation has been granted under a special act of parliament (Military Injury Act 1948) to more than 95,000 veterans suffering from permanent war injuries.

After World War II the Finnish State had limited resources to provide care for disabled war veterans. The greatest problems were caring for the dependants of around 94,000 fallen soldiers, the resettlement of half a million refugees from Karelia and the other areas lost during the war (innovation no. 66), and the payment of war reparations to Russia. Our government wanted to be very meticulous in fulfilling the peace treaty clause concerning war reparations between Finland and the Soviet Union in order to avoid occupation by or other pressures from her former enemy. It was for this reason that the Disabled War Veterans' Association had to create the system and build or buy the institutes for the care of its members by itself. Moreover, the association also had to finance itself by collecting money and soliciting donations. This was how the Kauniala Disabled War Veterans' Hospital started

1946. The association still runs the hospital today together with the City of Vantaa.

The rehabilitation system for disabled Finnish war veterans is highly esteemed internationally. On a worldwide scale, it was exceptional for a disabled war veterans' organisation to plan, create, partly finance and build the system and institutions for its own severely disabled members immediately after the war, when the state lacked sufficient resources to do it itself. The care and post-care of disabled war veterans has in many ways set the tone of Finnish social policy.

Finns think of the Winter War (1939–1940), the Continuation War (1941–1944) and the Lapland War (1944–1945) as defensive campaigns, so the sacrifices made in these wars are highly valued in the community. Before the Winter War disabled people in Finland had a poor status, but the positive attitude towards disabled war veterans was extended to include other disabled people. The Act on the Care of Disabled Civilians (1948) was drafted just after the war ended.

The path of disabled war veterans from war hospitals to convalescence and then on to returning to working life is one of the finest Finnish survival stories. Earlier, it would have been unthinkable for a severely disabled person to work and earn his living but the disabled war veterans themselves did not want to remain dependent on charity, and the fact was that the country needed all these people to work. They showed great resilience and generally managed to get along just as well as any able-bodied person.

Ordinary disabled rank-and-file war veterans founded the Disabled War Veterans' Association of Finland after the Winter War in 1940, strongly supported by Marshall Mannerheim, the Commander-in-Chief of the Armed

Forces. The organisation came into being at a time when young disabled men considered their position and future very uncertain, but they were bound together in a spirit of brotherhood born of their terrible experiences, both on the battlefield and in war hospitals.

The disabled war veterans themselves and their organisation provided the necessary services through developing new operations models and taking care of their implementation. Responsibility for financing the care was then transferred whenever possible to the state, which should have handled it from the very beginning. This is contrary to the government and municipalities' current practice of transferring the provision of health and social services to the so-called 'third sector' or private organisations.

Soon after the Winter War the Disabled War Veterans' Association joined forces with other organisations to initiate the vocational rehabilitation of disabled war veterans by setting up training courses and providing job placement services. Since the state had no plans for organising their long-term care, the association established the Kauniala treatment centre for veterans with spinal injuries, two treatment centres for those with brain injuries, and a vocational training centre for those suffering from war-induced tuberculosis. The Finnish Red Cross took care of the vocational training of veterans who had been blinded. The association founded a rehabilitation centre for war amputees in the 1950s, and training veterans to walk again and amputee veterans to use prostheses was later extended to include general rehabilitation aimed at helping veterans manage their daily lives. All these activities posed certain economic risks for the association, but it managed to carry them out successfully.

Neither social boundaries nor differences of opinion have disrupted the work of the association; its membership has included all disabled war veterans, irrespective of their political or other opinions. The association has also accepted veterans with minor injuries as members, and they have been able to contribute to helping their severely injured comrades. Today the widows and spouses of disabled war veterans also belong to the association. All in all it has become an organisation whose members, who represent different social circles, have always maintained a strong spirit of solidarity.

There are still 6,500 disabled war veterans alive in Finland today (September 2012). Nearly 80% of them live at home, despite an average age of over 88. The association's most important tasks today include improving their members' statutory treatment and compensation cover, as well as providing counselling services.

Nowadays the association, as an active voluntary organisation, is especially committed to providing support to help disabled war veterans, their spouses and widows to continue living at home by arranging home-help services and repairs to dwellings that are in poor condition. Close to 4,000 disabled war veterans, spouses and widows receive home care through the association's assistance project. This service includes daily household chores, gardening and outdoor work, and running errands, and social interaction is also an essential part of the service. The assistance project employs approximately 400 people with a history of long-term unemployment.

Veli-Matti Huittinen – Emeritus director of the Kauniala hospital for disabled war veterans

28. ABILIS FOUNDATION

Abilis Foundation's mission is to support disabled people and their organisations in developing countries. This does not sound particularly extraordinary, but the special importance of the Foundation will become apparent in due course.

In the early 1970s, university students, including myself, founded the disabled people's human rights organisation Threshold Association. Soon after this I travelled to the United States to get acquainted with the local disabled people's movement. I was overwhelmed when I saw how proud disabled people were of themselves. This had an enormous influence on a young man like me, and ever since I have considered international cooperation extremely important.

In 1980 Disabled Peoples' International (dpi) was founded, and I became an active participant. In 1990 I was elected dpi vice-president – with development as my main responsibility – and in 1994 I became president of the organisation.

The Finnish disabled people's organisations that are involved in development cooperation came together and founded Fidida, the Finnish Disabled People's International Development Association, which has with its affiliate organisations implemented and managed projects that support the disabled.

The Finnish government, i.e. the Ministry for Foreign Affairs, supported NGO projects by financing 80% of the accepted expenditure (currently 92.5% in projects targeted at disabled people). This system was excellent, but on the other hand very slow and rigid.

In developing countries I had seen how disabled people's organisations struggled with financial problems – just as the Threshold Association did in the beginning. I had also seen how big money (granted too easily at the wrong time) had destroyed several disabled people's associations. Large amounts of money granted by European organisations did not always lead to permanent changes, only corruption.

In the mid 1990s Pertti Paasio carried out an evaluation of the Finnish development cooperation, and one of his recommendations was the creation of new funding opportunities. I developed an idea for a Foundation that would directly support disabled people's organisations in developing countries and would be directly financed by the Finnish Ministry for Foreign Affairs. Pekka Haavisto, the minister responsible for development cooperation, supported the idea and sent me to meet his under-secretary Kirsti Lintonen. She said that the ministry would finance the foundation but first I had to find the basic capital.

I will not go into detail here about how we managed to get that capital, but it took time, energy, and plenty of friends and generous donations. But the money was collected, and the Abilis Foundation was founded.

The Foundation was formed by individuals. The majority of the board members are disabled themselves and disability activists, and the basic idea is for disabled people to help other disabled people. A foundation provides the best organisational structure because it focuses only on the activities defined in its charter, it cannot be taken over (unlike an association), and the money can only be used for what is described in the charter.

The Abilis Foundation naturally follows its own criteria concerning development aid. One fundamental part of its activities is providing small grants of up to 10,000 euros for disabled people's organisations in developing countries. Higher amounts are granted to organisations we have had good experiences with. Assistance is mainly provided on a one-off basis. We promote women's activities, human rights, education and projects that generate income.

The procedure is quite simple: a disabled people's organisation from a developing country contacts us, receives a application form, fills it in, and sends it back. Abilis Foundation checks that the applicant is genuine, and the board of directors decides, on the basis of the secretarial board's proposal, whether to support the project. The partner organisation is granted 50% of the total amount when the projects starts, 40% after the first project report, and 10% after the final project report.

It sounds easy, but given that applicants are practically grassroots organisations, there might be several difficulties, and lack of education and experience, in addition to the poor infrastructure in developing countries, may complicate the project. The Abilis Foundation helps its partner organisations cope with the necessary bureaucracy, and manuals written by the Foundation have been translated into several languages.

According to studies, the financial aid is mostly used for the purpose stated in the application. Small-scale benefits are achieved, but measuring them is a bit more complicated. A small village henhouse, a couple of cows for young disabled women, a training course on human rights, an internet cafe, etc; each and every result matters to individual disabled people and also to their organisations. According to our policy we finance a project only if disabled people participate in it from the very beginning. There are several projects financed by other organisations that support disabled people, but they do not participate in the planning and implementation of the project.

The Ministry for Foreign Affairs granted the Abilis Foundation 1 million euros in 2006 and 1.1 million euros in 2007. It is a large amount and it enables a lot; at the end of 2005 the Foundation was financing 170 projects in developing countries, and it currently employs five people in its Helsinki Office. It also has offices in India, Uganda, Kazakhstan and Nicaragua, and offices are presently being founded in Tanzania and probably Ethiopia. The offices in these cooperation countries are run by local people. The Foundation's activities will in the future concentrate on these countries, because its local partners can easily check that the applications are based on real needs, and that the projects are implemented. Nevertheless, we sometimes take risks and grant financial aid to difficult places – which are often the most needy.

State aid in 2012 amounted to 1.9 million euros, while in 2011 it was 1.8 million euros. In the coming years the budget and funding will rise to over 2 million euros. (NB! Applications for funding are currently dealt with by the Ministry for Foreign Affairs. The amount of funding applied for in 2013 is 2.7 million euros, and will be over 3 million euros the following year.)

There were a total of 250–280 applications last year. Usually we use an average figure of around 260. This is also true of the present situation (10/2012)

The foundation employs 9 full-time members of staff and two temporary employees. The number of employees will grow in accordance with the amount of work.

The Abilis foundation has 12 partner countries: Bangladesh, Ethiopia, India, Cambodia, Kazakhstan, the Kyrgyz Republic, Mozambique, Nepal, Somalia, Tadzikistan, Tanzania and Uganda. Preparations are also under way to begin cooperation with Zambia. The majority of project funding (60–70%) goes to those partner countries where the foundation has a cooperation organization (a local partner/partner organization) which makes sure that the applications are genuine and that the projects are realized.

Kalle Könkkölä – President of Abilis foundation, member of parliament 1983–1986

29 CAREGIVERS ALLOWANCE

Families and communities have participated in caring for the sick and disabled for as long as humans have existed, and although society has assumed responsibility for functions that were earlier shouldered almost entirely by the family and close friends, they still play a significant role as care providers; people receive an important part of the help and care they need from this source. This so-called informal care has a strong normative base due to its human indispensability and the feelings it involves.

The care provided by family members differs considerably from professional care in that the norms and agreements between family members, generations and genders are also present in the care they offer. Caring within the family is based on a special and unique personal relationship between individuals and the built-in obligation created by feelings and attachment. A close relationship is the most important motive and is an indispensable precondition for providing care. The relationship has not been formed by a need to care, but exists irrespective of it.

Nowadays the status of people who care for an old, disabled or sick person at home has come to be seen in a new light, and family care is perceived as a way of subsidising home care as a low-cost option which can replace intensive home or institutional care. In Finland the debate on family care started at the beginning of the 1980s with the introduction of a home care allowance for elderly and disabled people (Social Welfare Act), and it became a topic of real social interest in the 1990s when home and institutional care services were subject to cutbacks and support for informal care and assisted living was increased. Since 1993 the caregivers allowance has been a statutory social service which is governed by the Social Welfare Act and the Decree on Support for Informal Care. The Support for Informal Care Act came into effect at the beginning of 2006.

Support for informal care is defined in the care and service plan and includes the supply of services required by the invalid and compensation, leave and support services for the carer. The amount of compensation is set according to how binding and demanding the care is. The minimum allowance is 300 euros per month, and 600 euros per month during a transition period when the care is very demanding and the caregiver has to take temporary leave from his or her job. The family caregiver is entitled to at least two days leave per month when he or she is providing round-the-clock care. The caregiver's allowance can be claimed when

1. a person needs medical care or nursing due to impaired faculties, sickness, disability or similar, and a family member or close associate is prepared to take responsibility for their care with the help of the necessary services;
2. the health and ability of the caregiver fulfils the requirements for providing family care;
3. the provision of care, together with other necessary social and health services, is sufficient with regards to the well-being, health and security of the person being cared for;

4. the home of the person being cared for is suitable with regards to health and other conditions; or
5. the granting of support is considered to be in the best interests of the person being cared for. The actual amount of people participating in some level of family care is however considerably higher, although the exact figure would be difficult to estimate as there is no register. The numbers in Finland have been estimated at 150,000 people over 60 years old and 300,000 people of all age groups. Support for informal care is a systemic innovation from the 1980s which generates added value in the service system, and family care has become an essential part of the present system of caring for the elderly. The inclusion of the care given by one family member to another in the official social service system has made both the individuals concerned and society as a whole redefine their mutual rights and obligations. Family care is currently subject to active research and development, which is all to the good, and new methods to support care-giving families individually are being developed. Different kinds of organisations have a big part to play in this development work because versatile support for family carers requires multi-actor cooperation between municipalities, organisations, congregations and private service providers.

Päivi Voutilainen – Counciller of Social affairs, Ministry of Social Affairs and Health
Reija Heinola – Managing director, Central Union for the Welfare of the Aged

30 COMBATING POVERTY

Economic poverty has traditionally been a marginal phenomenon in the Finnish welfare model. Key strategies in combating poverty have included efforts to maintain a high level of employment and to prevent the risk of people ending up with inadequate income levels, in combination with income security and taxation policies that have been determinedly aimed at reducing income differentials.

Up to the late 1990s, earnings-related, contributory social security schemes were successful in ensuring reasonable consumption levels during interruptions in earned income. With longer periods of unemployment, however, masses of people fell from earnings-related income security to basic security. A major social policy issue at the turn of the millennium was therefore, somewhat surprisingly, the adequacy of basic security and the move to poverty policy; by poverty policy is meant the erosion of universalism while shifting towards residualism.

From a European and Nordic point of view, the gradual institutionalisation of minimum income security in Finland and the perception of minimum income as a fundamental social right is a significant social innovation.

In Finland, minimum income security consists of the minimum levels of situation-dependent social security (such as unemployment benefits), and social assistance in combination with housing allowance. All these benefits are statutory. The adequacy of the standard of living afforded by minimum income security can always be argued over. Living on minimum income security should always be seen as a temporary and short-lived phase.

The innovative element of basic security in Finland is legislative in origin. From 1983 onwards social assistance was gradually harmonised across the country. This implied that the use of discretion at the local level was gradually minimised. The reform of fundamental rights in 1995 was significant in this context. The right to basic security is enshrined in section 19 of the Constitution of Finland in a way that makes it a powerful, subjective right. Public authorities (municipalities) are obliged to provide statutory minimum income security to entitled citizens in all circumstances and whatever the reason for the need for support.

An increase in disparity in earnings and especially unemployment in the building industry has led to an increase in the number of homes with no wage-earners. Apart from the growth in poverty, the number of households in serious financial difficulties has grown in recent years, as have the length of queues for free bread. The provisions of the Constitution have been interpreted to imply that first-resort income security should be organised so that entitled citizens will have no need to seek social assistance. This is not always the case, however.

The lowest level of social security, that is, social assistance, represents the politico-administrative poverty line in Finland. It is Parliament's view of the level of material well-being below which nobody should need to fall.

In recent years, the minimum levels of social security have been clearly below the EU's risk of poverty line, which is 60 per cent of the median income. In Finland, this development is due to the pattern of income distribution and the growth of income differentials. The median income increases with the increasing prosperity of the majority of citizens, and so does the number of people at risk of poverty. This can be seen as poverty through income distribution.

Matti Heikkilä – Director general, STAKES 2008

31 GUARANTEE FOUNDATION

Even the Bible says that "the poor will always be with you", so what was it that mobilised the Evangelical-Lutheran Church of Finland at the end of the 1980s to develop new methods to help the poorest of the poor, i.e. people with histories of imprisonment, substance abuse, or institutionalisation? At that time there was a strong economic boom and everybody seemed to be doing incredibly well. But no, not quite everybody: those already in the margins were marginalised further – what bank would have wanted or needed an ex-convict for a client?

For this reason the Church proposed the creation of the Guarantee Foundation, which would offer to guarantee bank loans to combine several debts into one – it is much easier to manage one loan than several different debts, and the interest on a bank loan is cheaper than it is on debt-recovery proceedings. The Church's proposal was warmly received; the foundation was established by the Finnish Association for Mental Health, the A-Clinic Foundation and the Criminal Sanctions Agency, and the rules were agreed in record time.

But then their fortunes changed. The Church decided that funds for the new foundation and its guarantee fund would be provided by the Church Joint Responsibility Collection of 1991 (innovation no. 79), but people did not like the idea. Volunteers changed their minds ands refused to collect funds and donors disappeared. Roll up, ladies and gentlemen, now's your chance clear the debts of convicts and criminals! Be sure to give generously now! But the depression was starting and there were plenty other people who needed help, so the proceeds from the 1991 collection were considerably less than they had been in previous years.

Nevertheless, the Guarantee Foundation started to function in spring 1992. Trained contact people helped the clients by negotiating with the creditors to moderate the debts, and guarantees were offered to restructure the loans. Activities were conducted on a very small scale, but they did not go unnoticed. When it became evident that the Finnish Debt Restructuring Act of 1993 was causing major problems, especially for guarantors and families with small children, the Ministry of Social Affairs and Health inquired whether the Guarantee Foundation would be willing to expand its operations to offer guarantees to people from outwith special groups, and thus prevent debt problems spreading to affect people other than the debtors themselves. The proposal was accepted and the Foundation's operations expanded immensely. Its guarantees are currently very worthy of consideration as an aid to voluntary debt settlement; we estimate that around 30,000 Finns have beaten their debt problems with our help, and the sum total of debts settled with our guarantees exceeds one thousand million euros.

The Guarantee Foundation has also provided new methods for Finnish social administration. Social credit (innovation no. 32) started as our pilot project, but it is now encoded in the law. We participated in the development of a debt settlement project, which permitted approximately

10,000 excessively indebted persons to restructure their debts. In 1995 we started a toll-free Advisory Debt Line, which provides "first-aid" help for excessively indebted people and directs them to the right services. We have a good vantage point and have thus been able to foresee the future causes of debt problems, such as text message payday loans or excessively long or large mortgages. Finnish debts have doubled since 2002. Especially 25–34-year-olds' mortgages are large, around 120,000 euros on average. Ways of getting into debt have changed, however, and the biggest problems nowadays are caused by payday loans that can be secured with an SMS from a mobile phone, and the number of these being accessed has grown massively. In 2001 loans to the value of 320 million euros were granted in this manner: around 1.4 million separate loans. The size of the average payday loan is 240 euros and the average time to repay it is 34 days. The annual interest on these loans is over 1000%. This can lead to repayment difficulties, and default increased by 25% in 2012. A law is being processed in the parliament to regulate payday loans with regards to their interest rates and maximum commissions.

There are probably no organisations like the Guarantee Foundation anywhere else in the world, as we know from the number of times that we have been invited abroad to talk about our activities. It has been a pleasure to do so, and the results speak for themselves. As our founding constitution states, The Other Side of Justice is Moderation.

Leena Veikkola – Operations manager,
Guarantee foundation 1991–2012

32 SOCIAL CREDIT

In the 1990s legislative means were used in Finland to help those who had accrued excessive debts during the economic depression. The Finnish Debt Settlement Act came into effect in 1993. However, it was later noted that voluntary debt settlement resources, such as economic counselling and social credit, were also needed to solve and prevent debt problems.

In 1999–2001 the Ministry of Social Affairs and Health implemented a Social Credit Pilot Project in eight municipalities. The results indicated that social credit can prevent economic marginalisation and excessive debts in households with low incomes and limited means, and also promote the independence of the family.

In three years the Pilot Project granted more than 1,100 credit payments, amounting to over 3 million euros. The project researchers estimated that credit losses occurred in approximately 5% of cases, but part of this could be covered with interest payments. For example, in Helsinki the income from interest was 176,000 euros, while credit losses were 101,000 euros in total.

The Social Credit Act came into effect on 1 January 2003. Amendments were made to the Social Welfare Act and the Act on the Status and Rights of Social Welfare Clients by including clauses relating to social credit.

Municipalities (innovation no. 4) have the power to grant social credit as part of social welfare to inhabitants who have no other way of getting credit on reasonable terms, e.g. because they have defaulted on previous credit contracts, or have a low income or limited means. Credit can be issued for debt restructuring, household purchases and renovations, or as a student loan for those who do not qualify for a state guarantee for a student loan because they have defaulted on previous credit payments.

However, social credit cannot be issued as a substitute for any social assistance that the client is entitled to.

In Helsinki the social administration has issued social credit since 1999 – first as part of the Pilot Project and since 2003 as permanent statutory activity. Credit is a means of restoring clients' independence in the form of social assistance. According to calculations, social assistance savings are considerably higher than the operating and credit loss costs of the social credit programme. Credit is issued by the social administration's economic and debt counselling department, and it is included in the individual person's voluntary debt settlement. The debtor is thus provided with flexible economic counselling, especially when there are problems with debt repayment. The maximum loan is 10,000 euros and the maximum repayment period is five years. The client pays interest according to the 12-month Euribor index. There are no other expenses.

Repayment problems regarding consumer loans have increased in Finland. Social credit is an important means of helping to solve the debt problems of households with low incomes or limited means. Often they are the ones who have to pay the highest price for consumer loans.

Marianne Rikama – Director, Helsinki social services department

33 STATE ALCOHOL MONOPOLY

Finland established a state alcohol monopoly in 1932, after prohibition (1919–1932) ended when it was rejected in a referendum in 1931. The state alcohol monopoly has not only been a Finnish innovation; similar monopolies can be found in the other Nordic countries except Denmark, in a number of states in the USA, and in some provinces of Canada. What is peculiar to Finland is what happened before and after the establishment of such a monopoly.

The idea behind a state alcohol monopoly is the belief that alcohol-related harm can be effectively regulated by controlling the availability of alcoholic beverages. In many countries, at different times, a state monopoly has been an effective means of regulating the aggregate alcohol consumption, and thereby decreasing alcoholrelated public health problems to the benefit of social relations and public order. There is a vast amount of research literature to support this view. Other arguments in favour of the monopoly included the elimination of private profit from the manufacture and sale of a potentially detrimental commodity, and the hidden arguments of monopoly as an effective tax-collecting tool and as a means to respond to some industrial policy problems played a role in the early stages.

Prior to the opening of monopoly shops on 5 April 1932 at 10 o'clock (note the countdown 5 4 3 2 1 0), Finland enjoyed 13 years of prohibition. The Prohibition Act was approved by Finland's first modern democratic Parliament in 1907 (innovation no. 1), but due to various delays in the Imperial Russian administration, to which Finland was bound as a part of the Russian Empire, it was not enforced until 1919, after Finland had gained her independence. The experience of prohibition was mixed. Negative aspects included an increase in smuggling and organised crime, together with a rise in crime in general, but on the plus side there were some, although not too many, improvements in general health and social life. One reason for the lack of dramatic improvements may be that alcohol consumption was at a low level in Finland already before prohibition was introduced.

After the establishment of the monopoly the availability of alcohol was restricted, especially in the countryside where there were no monopoly stores. The exceptional conditions produced by the Second World War led to a special system to control individual consumers' purchases. This, like any other monopoly activity, was based on the belief that control is a good way to prevent problems. After more than 10 years of client control the system was abandoned after studies showed that its effects were negligible. The next major innovation within the monopoly system was the alcohol reform of 1969, which included the creation of a new outlet for beer, which could now be purchased from grocery stores and cafés, and the granting of permission for monopoly stores to open up in the countryside. The reform resulted in a gigantic increase in alcohol consumption and alcohol-related harm in the 1970s, an event that surprised all the planners and showed that the control of availability of alcoholic beverages has a strong impact on the prevention of alcohol-related harm. It was however politically impossible to return to a more restrictive control system.

Today the Finnish State Alcohol Monopoly has even survived the country joining the EU in 1995, gaining official acceptance in Brussels on the basis that its aim is to protect public health. There has been continuous pressure towards a further liberalisation of the system, e.g. allowing wine to be sold in grocery stores, but no big changes have been implemented so far. The alcohol issue was back on the public agenda again with the alcohol taxation reform of 2004, in which Finland found it necessary to lower alcohol taxes due to Estonia joining the EU and also because EU rules required a more liberal policy on tourist importation of alcohol. Alcohol consumption and alcohol-related harm consequently leaped upwards, causing much concern among the general public and politicians.

The importance of the alcohol issue in Finnish politics is revealed by the fact that there have been only two referendums in the country since it became independent in 1917. The first one was in 1931 on prohibition, and the second one on EU membership in 1994. The monopoly system has faced many new challenges in the globalisation process, but it has survived, even though Finland is now an EU member country.

Jussi Simpura – Head of division, Director of National Institute for Health and Welfare

34 NOVEMBER MOVEMENT

Finland has always had a strict control system and a very institutions-oriented policy. In the 1960s Finland had four times more prisoners than the other Nordic countries despite a comparable crime rate. 0.4% of the population were institutionalised in mental hospitals, the joint highest number in the world with Ireland and Sweden, and the number of detentions for drunkenness was ten times higher than it was in Denmark. Conscientious objectors, including Jehovah Witnesses, served 2 years and 7 months in a closed camp, homosexuality was illegal, people with unpaid child support payments were sent to labour camps as vagrants, and alcoholics' institutions were based on compulsory treatment. Institutional discipline was extreme, even in the reform schools, and there was a lot of homelessness.

Social scientists around the world published books and articles on the sociology of deviant behaviour, which was mainly directed at the controlled groups mentioned above. Startling research articles were also published in Finland, especially by the Finnish Foundation for Alcohol Studies and the Finnish Research Institute for Criminology. In 1966 the University of Helsinki Student Union (innovation no. 73) organised a series of five panel discussions about e.g. prisoners, people with mental health problems, vagrants, work-shy or homeless people and alcoholics, and a new wave of polemic pamphlets also began to appear. A group of sociologists, lawyers, writers and physicians published a book on compulsory treatment (Pakkoauttajat, (Beware of Care)), edited by Lars D. Eriksson. The book really put the cat among the pigeons and set the scene for an intensive debate in the media about institutions and compulsory treatment, and the prevailing social welfare and control policy received a lot of criticism. Radical associations had already been founded in other Nordic countries to defend prisoners' interests.

On 7 November 1967 a Finnish control policy association, the November Movement, was founded to help improve the standing of all the groups mentioned above. The development of the association got a boost from a national scandal when 40 homeless people died of exposure due to the closing of a 500-bed night shelter earlier that year, and it gained a lot of publicity on 6 December 1967, the 50th anniversary celebration of independent Finland – at the same time as President Kekkonen was hosting a party for the county's elite at the presidential palace, the November Movement invited all of Helsinki's homeless people to the Student House for sausages and beer. Around 500 men came to hear the rousing speeches and protest songs, and the event received as much if not more attention as the president's gala. There were three stewards at the event, including Paavo Lipponen, who later became the Finnish Prime Minister and Speaker of the Parliament. A short time earlier an abandoned paint warehouse had been transformed into a 1000-bed night shelter, where society's most marginalised members slept in coffin-like wooden boxes. The country was celebrating, but the misery was palpable. On Independence Day the November

Movement also published its list of the 50 evils of Finnish society.

The Movement was divided into three fieldrelated working groups which organised demonstrations, compiled background information, wrote memoranda, edited books, started research projects and established shadow committees. Proper public committees were also established, most importantly the Committee for the Basis of Social Welfare, and the members also succeeded to some extent in realising their plans to take over leading positions in public administration. They invited artists and politicians to institutions and organised debates before the upcoming election.

People who were subject to institutional control and domination also participated in the movement, although most of its thousand members were young academics.

The November Movement was one of the most visible Finnish single-issue movements in the 1960s, along with the unilateral nuclear disarmament peace organisation the Committee of 100; Yhdistys 9, which mapped gender roles; the pro-Third World movement Tricont; and the Traffic Policy Association called Marjority, which criticised the prevailing car culture and promoted efficient public transport and better conditions for pedestrians and cyclists.

The November Movement was active from 1967 to 1971, during which time its aim was to promote the foundation of specific interest organisations (innovation no. 68). This resulted in the founding of the Finnish Gypsy Union in 1967; the Finnish Conscript Union, the sexual equality organisation Seta and the Organisation for Psychiatric Rehabilitation in 1970; the Finnish Central Association for Mental Health in 1971; and the Union of Conscientious

Objectors in 1974. It took a little bit longer before the Homeless People's Association and the Y-Foundation, which constructs and provides accommodation for needy single people (innovation no. 16), were founded.

Klaus Mäkelä, the author of the movement's declaration of principles, has stated: "The salient principles of the movement illustrate not only social indignation, but also a strong, social scientific belief in reason. Many of the activists were affiliated to political parties, but the movement itself was clearly independent."

He continues however: "in the ideological seminar organised in autumn 1969 the younger generation criticised the older one for petty bourgeois reformism in a manner that anticipated, in many respects, the forthcoming confrontations of the 1970s." The new generation wanted to eradicate poverty from the whole world instead of merely tinkering with Finns living in extreme poverty (innovation no. 30).

The November Movement was wound up in 1972 as it had accomplished its mission. It had mobilised new organisations, influenced the public authorities and changed public opinion.

Ilkka Taipale – Member of parliament 1971–1975, 2000–2007

35 THREE PERCENT THEORY

Before participating in the police department's second homicide seminar in Aulanko in 1993 I read all the Finnish literature I could find on the subject, apart from detective novels. Government Councillor Jussi Pajuoja from the Ministry of Justice had observed that twothirds of the approximately 160 annual homicides in Finland were committed by people that belonged to a group which represented 5% of Finnish men who were unemployed even during times of economic prosperity when there was plenty of work around. If we remove groups that do not tend to kill others, e. g. Swedish-speakers (innovation no. 11), Laestadian Lutherans, peaceful mental patients and pensioners that either belong to the first or second social class or are mentally handicapped or disabled, we are left with 3% of Finnish men. This group consists of 40,000 men, most of whom are single or divorced and live alone.

So who are these people? Practically speaking, all of Finland's homeless people (80% of whom are men) and prisoners (97% men) belong to this group, along with former reform school students, army rejects, long-term unemployed people who didn't work even during the economic boom, degenerate alcoholics and the majority of drug addicts. A person from a poor and quarrelsome family who suffers from mbd (Minimal Brain Dysfunction), adhd (Attention-Deficit Hyperactivity Disorder) or difficult dyslexia, or is of limited intelligence, also has a good chance of ending up in this group.

This small group of people not only commit murders but place a lot of strain on our society by e.g. burdening the police and judicial authorities as well as social welfare and health care through the trouble they cause and the illnesses they suffer from.

The Finnish Ministry of the Interior recently analysed the major security threats in Finland, and found that these come not from computer hackers, bird flu, hiv, Russian criminals or global warming, but poor and lonely 20–40-yearolds who expect nothing from society (and from whom society expects nothing in return).

These men are serviced by around 20,000 paid workers: special education teachers, social workers, carers and nurses, doctors, ambulance drivers, policemen, prison guards, porters, cleaners, firemen, clergymen and a whole army of e.g. voluntary AA men and support people, but nothing seems to help. While older men quieten down and die off, there are always others growing up to replace them.

What actually happens to this group? According to Professor Tapani Valkonen, we are now seeing the fourth mortality wave in Finland. First the men died in the war (every sixth participant), then until the mid-1950s it was tb, and after that came cardiovascular disease (innovation no. 43). Now poor men under 45 are dying but, says Valkonen, "not by being chopped down by the Grim Reaper but under the mowing machine". Pekka Karhunen, a professor of forensic medicine, has also stated that "there are too many young men on the table". They die of e.g. fatal wounds, accidents, suicide, intoxication and tobacco and alcohol-related diseases. However, there is one major difference: the first three trends affected both rich and poor, so there was a general interest in solving the problem, but now that only poor people are dying it seems that no one really cares about pawns that are no longer part of the game.

According to the 3% theory, focusing a strong measure of Bismarckian social policy on this residual group would do a lot to solve the problem. We have numerous examples of miniature societies: when people are treated well they respond in kind.

Up until 1995 Finland was the only European country in which the number of both homeless people and prisoners was declining.

If we want to preserve our social harmony we must make considerable improvements to the social status of this troubling group. In symbolic terms, if rich and poor cannot look each other in the eye, it will be an eye for an eye.

Even the police estimate that the number of murders could be cut by 35%. Although the number has declined by one-third since the 1930s, it is still three to five times greater than many other European countries.

Certain things must be done to remedy this situation: first of all we must construct small flats and service homes to reduce and ultimately eradicate homelessness (innovations nos. 16 and 18); secondly, a special pension must be granted to the disabled; thirdly, income-related poverty must be eliminated (innovation no. 30); and fourthly, special recreational and leisure time as well as work-related activities must be intensified, and the youth workshop network must be expanded.

The costs of these measures are considerably lower than the current cost of the trouble caused by this group.

Ilkka Taipale – Member of parliament 1971–1975, 2000–2007

36 LEGAL AID AND CRIMINAL DAMAGE COMPENSATION

According to educational ideals, international human rights conventions and the Finnish Constitution, all persons are equal before the law. This fundamental right is not fulfilled if in reality a person cannot afford to take a matter to court or to defend himor herself in court with the help of a competent professional. This is why we consider it important in Finland that we have a system of legal aid and compensation for victims of crime that stands up to international comparison.

Legal aid began to be developed in Finland in the late nineteenth century, when certain discerning members of the gentility considered it an injustice that the poorer echelons of society could not even dream of taking their matters to an expensive court. The City of Helsinki initiated a legal aid system in 1886, and a legal aid office has been operational in Helsinki since then. The first law on public legal aid was passed in 1973. In 1998, the responsibility for legal aid actions was transferred from municipal councils to the government, and in a legal reform of 2002, legal aid was extended to apply not only to persons of limited means but also to a significant proportion of people of average income.

Today, legal aid can be granted for almost all legal cases, with the exception of exiguous cases and cases covered by legal expenses insurance. Legal aid means that persons (not companies or corporations) resident in Finland receive assistance for conducting a legal case in the form of a legal counsel whose expenses are wholly or partly covered by the state. More detailed information on the income limits for receiving complete or partial legal aid can be found on the Ministry of Justice website and at legal aid offices.

In certain cases, the criminally accused are guaranteed a defence regardless of income level. Similarly, victims of serious violent crime and sexual offences may be appointed a state-funded legal counsel or support person regardless of their income level. Contrary to popular belief, in international terms, Finland has an unusually extensive compensation and aid system to help even the victims of many other crimes. The Act on Compensation for Crime Damage was recently amended (in 2006), increasing the rights of victims of grave violent crime and sexual offences, in particular, to receive compensation from the state for damages and – in an important new addition – also for mental suffering.

Even though Finland is at the forefront, globally speaking, of public legal aid and assistance and compensation for victims of crime, both systems still have room for improvement. When the Legal Aid Act was last amended, some Members of Parliament expressed concerns that, despite its intentions, the reform did not improve the middle classes' opportunities for taking matters to court because legal aid does not cover the injunction to pay the often very costly legal expenses of the adverse party, which usually befalls the losing party. The Parliament (innovation no. 1) was also concerned that the lack of funds for legal aid would in reality lead to a "zero-sum game", in which extending legal aid to cover the middle classes would mean excluding people of more limited means. The reform was also criticised for making the distribution of work between lawyers and legal counsels somewhat inefficient.

Feedback from citizens and preliminary enquiries made by the National Research Institute of Legal Policy into the legal reform have indicated that the concerns expressed by the Parliament were not unfounded. In short, the legal aid and criminal compensation systems lack money. Budgetary allocations to judicial administration have been inexplicably low in recent years, and this is reflected in everyday complications in these fine instruments of justice, as well as in surprisingly large deductibles that the persons entitled to aid or compensation must personally cover.

Tuija Brax – Minister of Justice 2007–2011

37 VICTIM–OFFENDER MEDIATION IN CRIMINAL MATTERS

Finland was among the first countries in Europe to pilot victim–offender mediation in criminal matters and minor disputes with its project in the city of Vantaa in 1983. The pilot was regarded as necessary for two reasons. Criminal policy in Finland was dominated by what is called the neoclassical theory of criminal justice, where the emphasis was on punishing offenders on the basis of their acts alone. Personal qualities or social status had no significance in assessing guilt. This focus on criminal acts largely deprived the Finnish criminal policy of alternative approaches. Unlike elsewhere in Europe, no alternative sanctions were made extensively available to young offenders, for example. The mediation model that was applied in Vantaa had unexpectedly positive results. As a result of the favourable publicity received, the activities were made a permanent part of municipal social work. The model also spread rapidly to other large cities in Finland.

Co-operation between the authorities and municipal mediation offices has been active. More than 80 per cent of all cases have been referred to mediation by the police and prosecution authorities. Dispute resolutions have represented some 5 per cent. Young people have accounted for 55 per cent, and what is significant is that children under 15, i.e. under the age of penal responsibility, have accounted for 15 per cent of all mediation cases over the years. In the case of children, mediation is an excellent method of early intervention. The younger the person participating in the process is, the more mediation curbs recidivism. Mediation has been well received: 75 per cent of the parties referred to mediation have agreed to the process and 90 per cent of the resulting agreements have been fulfilled. The offenders have been satisfied with the mediation in more than 80 per cent and the victims in 75 per cent of the cases. Success rates are high even by international comparison.

Currently between 3,500 and 4,000 cases are referred to mediation each year.

In 1995, due to the economic recession, the mediation activities launched by local authorities on a voluntary basis were partly suspended and even terminated. As research findings confirmed the significance of mediation activities, persistent efforts were made to make the activities a nationwide practice funded from the state budget and with a statutory basis. In autumn 2005, Parliament (innovation no. 1) adopted a new act on mediation in criminal matters and minor disputes, granting 6.3 million euros annually for implementation at the national level. The new act provides all citizens with the right and opportunity to participate in mediation concerning their offence or minor dispute.

The implementation of the act is co-ordinated by the Ministry of Social Affairs and Health. The State Provincial Offices ensure the availability of mediation services in all parts of the country by concluding commission agreements with local authorities, businesses in the social sector and possibly private providers of mediation services. The Research and Development Centre for Welfare and Health carries out research on the implementation and outcomes of the new act.

Juhani Iivari – Adjunct Professor, Head of Research at the National Institute for Health and Welfare

HEALTH

38 ALL-INCLUSIVE HEALTH CENTRES

When it comes to Primary Health Care solutions, Finland stands almost alone. The whole population is covered by a network of about 275 local municipal Primary Health Care centres, which provide a wide range of preventive and curative primary-level services. General Practitioners, nurses, public health nurses working in preventive services, dentists, physiotherapists, psychologists and many other professions comprise highly diverse, and also large (per catchment population) multi-task professional teams. In addition to outpatient care, Finnish health centres even have GP-run hospital units, which offer both long-term and acute or short-term care to those who do not need highly specialised treatment.

Looking back, Finnish health centre is truly an innovation. It began with a law that was passed in 1972 requiring municipalities to provide a wide range of services, with the ambitious goal of merging public health activities and clinical services on a local level. The architects of the system were actually young radical medical doctors who, in the spirit of the 1960s and '70s, felt that traditional office-based medical practice was not the right answer to Finnish health problems at that time. The era was epidemiologically remarkable; Finland had successfully overcome tuberculosis and other contagious diseases, but young adults, especially in the Eastern and Northern parts of the country, were dying of heart disease. This was also a time when there was great optimism about the power of prevention – cancer screening had shown great results and was seen as a tool that would have an increasingly positive impact on the health of the population.

The first health centres, which were built as innovative pilot sites before the 1972 law came into effect, were buildings with facilities to accommodate the needs of various health professionals and parallel services. Interestingly, the first buildings had several office rooms which were designated "screening rooms". The buildings housed general practitioners, public health nurses, dentists, and, from older times, GP-run hospitals. In preceding decades these hospitals had served the country's rural areas – GP's in the 1950s had to be brave surgeons, obstetricians, and be able to cater for all kinds of health needs, but the new GP-run hospitals soon gave up major surgical operations and, with the exception of some centres in very remote areas, obstetric services too. Older people came instead for short or long-term care. Even now, for every 1 000 Finns there is an average of 4.4 GP-run hospital beds, out of which 2.4 are for short-stay care. This is a unique feature which has an uncertain future some see these hospitals as old-fashioned excess while others regard them as a useful tool that enables modern specialist hospitals to offer an efficient short-stay service.

Since health centres were launched in 1972 they have received substantial state subsidies for both building new facilities and expanding their range of services by adding new professionals to their ranks. New types of service have become available since it all began 34 years ago. The core tasks of the Finnish health centres are the following:

- Serving its catchment area with preventive services and health promotion (including antenatal care, healthy child care, school health, etc.)
- GP-level diagnostic and curative services, now often by a team of GP's and nurses
- Dental care
- GP-run hospital services
- Home nursing
- Mental health care (often divided at some line with specialist-level services)
- Rehabilitation services (physiotherapy, post-operative rehabilitation, physical aids, etc.)
- Organisation of ambulance services (often operated by private entrepreneurs from the fire department)
- Provision of occupational health services to employers (and their employees) and to self-employed persons
- Environmental health / health protection (food and water hygiene etc., combating epidemics)
- Student health care (innovation no. 40)

Finnish health centres have not always basked in such popularity – at first they were viewed with suspicion as instruments to interfere with private practitioners' entrepreneurial services. Indeed some municipal GP's, who had been essentially private practitioners with a special contract with the local authority, felt that they could not change to working as salaried professionals.

During the first 10–20 years of constructing the facilities and professional personnel, key elements of user-friendliness were unfortunately passed over. Access to the GP, telephone services and at times also the general atmosphere in health centres have left room for improvement, but these problems have now been tackled through national measures. In order to improve both access to and continuity of care, GP's were given the opportunity to compile a personal patient list instead of serving random residents of the municipality. This new model was soon applied to almost 75% of the population, especially in urban areas where service had been too unresponsive and impersonal. Later, in the 2000s, in the country of the mobile phone, it was discovered that health centres were too often unreachable by telephone. In 2002 a special addition was made to the primary care law: health centres must answer the telephone and a health professional must assess the patient within three working days, even in non-urgent cases.

Over the last 13 years health centres have become much more heterogeneous due to a shift towards decentralised administration, which was brought about by legislation that came into effect in 1993. Health centres can now function as integrated service sites for social welfare and primary health care needs. In some cases local specialist hospitals have been administratively and also functionally merged with primary health care administration and health centres, an innovation that even critics see as something that will help meet the challenges that will be faced in the coming decades.

Simo Kokko – Head of Development at the National Institute for Health and Welfare

39 MATERNITY AND WELL-BABY CLINICS

Childbirth was a dangerous thing a hundred years ago, a time when 1 in 170 births in Finland ended in maternal death and 3 babies in 100 were stillborn. On top of that, 15% of children died before their first birthday. Of 9 children born in the early 1890s into a farming family in the prosperous community of Urjala, 1 was stillborn, 3 died in infancy, and whooping cough took another at 3 years of age. The youngest, who survived, became a district nurse, or 'health sister'.

The first maternity and well-baby clinics were opened in Paris in the 1890s with the aim of supporting pregnant women and improving infants' nutrition. The idea arrived in Finland with General Mannerheim's League for Child Protection, a charity which, in the 1920s, invited the German-trained paediatrician Arvo Ylppö to become the director of its hospital. Ylppö accepted and started additional training for nurses, providing them with the skills to advise mothers in infant and child care. Similar training in Swedish was arranged by another charity, Samfundet Folkhälsan, first in the form of an apprenticeship and from 1927 through courses. The Finnish state assumed responsibility for training health sisters in 1931, while the hiring of midwives was the first communal health care activity to receive state funding.

The first well-baby clinic in Finland was opened in 1922 and the first maternity care clinic in 1926. Both activities have to this day remained part of primary care, outwith hospitals. These expanded slowly through charitable support until some communities started setting up clinics too; legislation in 1944 then required all local communities to set up free maternity and well-baby clinics. Maternal mortality had by this time decreased to 1 in 2,500 deliveries and infant mortality was under 6%. The infant mortality rate continued its downward trend, falling to 2% in the 1960s. Foreign physicians who were visiting Finland at the time wondered how this was possible when the physician to population ratio was the third lowest in Europe, but our secrets were the health sisters and district midwives who ran the well-baby and maternity clinics, consulting the general practitioner as required. District nurses and midwives also made home visits and were thus familiar with the families' living conditions.

Maternity clinics began to provide fitness classes for pregnant women in the late 1940s to prepare them for the hardships of labour and delivery. Psychological training was added in the 1960s and fathers were invited to join antenatal classes in the 1970s. Pregnancy was monitored in many ways, the oldest guidelines being weight, blood pressure, oedema, haemoglobin and urinary sugar and protein. The range of diseases that can be found and treated had widened from syphilis and tuberculosis, with professionals now able to look for Rhesus antibodies, hiv, and foetal structural abnormalities. Nutritional advice and help in quitting smoking have also supported a favourable course of pregnancy.

Nearly all mothers visited maternity clinics – partly motivated by the maternity pack (innovation no. 25) – but only in the late 1950s did the well-baby clinics succeed in recruiting enough health sisters to fully cover the demand. In addition to advising mothers and following the child's development, well-baby clinics were also responsible for vaccinations; although the national vaccination programme has never been compulsory, over 95% of Finnish children have over the years been vaccinated against all the diseases in the programme before they go to school.

In 2000 the Finnish infant mortality rate dropped below 0.6%, and maternal death occurs in less than 1 delivery in 6,000. Reasons for this include an overall increase in wealth and progress in health care, but one essential factor has certainly been the health-promoting work of maternal and well-baby clinics, free of charge and open to all, where trained and dedicated health sisters screen for disease and provide advice on child care and healthy lifestyles. The population has used these services, irrespective of where they have lived or what level of education they have had.

Marjukka Mäkelä – Research Professor at the National Institute for Health and Welfare

40 FINNISH STUDENT HEALTH SERVICE

The Finnish Student Health Service (FSHS) provides university students and high school students with health and medical care, as well as mental health and dental services. The system may be used by all undergraduate students. The fact that university students have their own health care system is a special feature of Finland's health care system.

FSHS specializes in student health care and offers all Finnish university undergraduates health care services in their own municipality. FSHS is funded by the National Centre for Pensions, students, student unions and the Ministry of Education and is a recognized part of the Finnish health care system.

The core function of FSHS is to maintain and improve the students' capacity to study by promoting students' health and preventing and treating diseases. The decision to have a separate health care system for university students is based on the fact that as young adults they have specific health care needs, and the services are geared to serve mental health, dentistry and sexual and reproductive health. All FSHS activities are based on a thorough understanding of students' health care needs. Active student participation supports the service and they have a say in the decision-making process and in evaluating and developing the way it works.

The service was founded in 1954 by the Finnish Student Union (SYL) as a result of a growing interest in developing student health care. The beginning of this can be dated to 1932, when the Finnish Anti-Tuberculosis Association began to examine students' lungs. In 1945 SYL set up a new committee on student health care to analyse how student health and medical care could be organised after an earlier attempt had failed during the war. SYL decided to commence activity the same year.

SYL's student health care office opened its doors in 1946 and concentrated its activities on checks for TB and treating illness. The head doctor was Dr Göta Tingvald Hannikainen. At the same time The Finnish Association to Prevent Sexually-transmitted Disease funded screening for syphilis. These early projects are a good demonstration of the nature of the service, which has has since the beginning focused on what young adults need.

Funding was secured in 1947 when the Finnish Parliament (innovation no. 1) enacted a law on the compulsory medical examination of university students and set an obligatory health care fee for each term. The functions of the Student Health Care Office were later transferred to the new FSHS foundation, which started to apply for funding also from Finland's Slot Machine Association (innovation no. 70) and asked the universities to provide the necessary premises. In 1955 the state budget included an allocation to fund the FSHS for the first time, and a student health association was founded in 1956 to seek more financial support.

University students' health care services have since been the responsibility of the foundation, although in the 1970s it was widely debated whether they should be transferred to the municipalities. There has been discussion about whether FSHS's services should also be available to polytechnic students ever since these schools were created. After a great deal of considerationa three-year trial began in 2011 with polytechnic students from schools in Saimaa, Lapeenranta and Seinäjoki.

FSHS has remained responsible for student health care because there are clear and simple grounds for its functions and activities.

Vesa Vuorenkoski – Member of FSHS board of directors 2004–2005

41 THE FINNISH INSTITUTE OF OCCUPATIONAL HEALTH

The Finnish Institute of Occupational Health (FIOH) was founded nearly 70 years ago in a fairly short time-span. At the end of 1944 Dr Leo Noro and Professor Arvo Vesa presented their concerns about the rise in occupational disease to the National Board of Health. They saw great opportunities for the development of occupational health practice, and Noro was particularly interested in the connections between work and health, having as a doctor seen cases of e.g. drivers exposed to wood gas generators and yellow-skinned ammunition loaders who were suffering from liver disease.

The National Board of Health set up a committee at the beginning of January 1945 to find a way to promote research on occupational disease. The committee completed its work by February, and on 4.4.1945 an occupational disease ward was opened in Helsinki General Hospital. The original staff consisted of three doctors, three nurses and two cleaners.

Being such a small occupational disease unit, however, it was unable to produce the research information needed to effectively prevent and control occupational disease. Noro envisioned an institute in which multidisciplinary specialists would study working life phenomena, and which would provide training for occupational groups, study patients and disseminate information. This institute would effectively convert theoretical expertise into practical use for the worker's benefit.

The institute needed support and funding, so many bodies concerned with work-related research and illness came on board: state authorities, representatives of industry, insurance companies and labour market organisations.

The fioh began its work with enthusiasm and open-mindedness. International arenas provided many new tools for research such as toxicology, epidemiology, biotechnology (later known as ergonomics), occupational psychology and occupational safety. Some of the latest activities have centred around research into the health effects of nano particles and applications such as chronophysiology and neuroergonomics, which have made it possible to research the effects of work schedule arrangements on general well being and the information load on the brain.

Occupational health activities also assumed new forms. Initially the main concern was serious exposure to poisonous substances, but over the decades chronic diseases, measurement of exposure to substances, preventative activities, health promotion, maintenance of work ability and general well being have risen to the fore.

From a unit comprising only a few experts, the fioh has grown into a multidisciplinary research and specialist institute, actively working to develop its field in Finland and in EU and UN organisations. The fioh has played a definitive role in Finnish occupational health and safety legislation and in the development of occupational health services. The current laws on occupational safety define its general aims and emphasise initiative in safety management at the workplace. For its part, the law on occupational health requires the employer to organise preventative health services for its employees.

About 90% of employees are now covered by occupational health services; the remaining 10% consist mainly of those working for small enterprises. The influence of the fioh can also be seen in e.g. the occupational safety and health strategies of the WHO and ILO.

Occasionally we at the fioh have become so engrossed in research that the actual development of working life has taken a back seat. However, the fioh is now back on track, developing solutions for the improvement of occupational health and well being together with its clients and partners. In this way the fioh promotes occupational health and safety as part of good living. Special attention needs to be paid to the globalisation of working life, the ageing workforce, coping at work in the midst of change and uncertainty, the health effects of new technologies (such as nano-, bioand genetic technology), the increase of allergies in working life and the work/life balance.

Harri Vainio – Director general of Institute of Occupational Health

42 HALVING THE NUMBER OF ROAD DEATHS

Traffic safety, especially with regards to road traffic, has been a major problem in Finland for a long time, even though the media is much more concerned with major aeroplane accidents and car crashes. Up until the 1960s, although there had been some research on the theme, there had not been much action in the way of legislation, information campaigns or public debate.

Only when statistics published at the end of the 1960s demonstrated that the situation was not only getting worse, but that Finland was close to becoming Europe's traffic black-spot, did politicians wake up to the problem. In spring 1972 the Government (innovation no. 5) appointed a Parliamentary Traffic Committee, which created a special Traffic Safety Division. At that time there were around 1,200 road casualties annually in Finland.

And that is how it all started. Not because of an individual accident, an especially eager state official or a career-minded politician; not even because of President Kekkonen's New Year speech. Everyone contributed, and the best thing was the good spirit and cooperation that existed within the Traffic Safety Division. I am proud that I was able to participate in this process, which has saved thousands of lives and spared plenty of sorrow, grief, pain and expenses.

Our first accomplishment was a general speed limit for each type of road. I can still remember how the president of the Central Union of Agricultural Producers and Forest Owners charged into my office, shouting that Helsinki would be left without fresh milk if my proposal was approved. There is still fresh milk on every breakfast table in Finland, but speeders have had to curb their reckless driving.

The general speed limit was accepted, partly because of the first oil crisis, but our proposal on compulsory seatbelts caused an even bigger commotion. Despite extremely convincing international data, there was strong opposition in the Parliament (innovation no. 1) among all the parties. Some people actually wanted to see me stand trial in the High Court of Impeachment because of my "anti-liberal" intentions. Finally, I invited my adversaries to a hospital to see the multiple injuries of patients who had neglected to use their seatbelts. That worked, and the bill passed with a clear majority in a parliamentary plenary session.

The number of road casualties fell rapidly, mainly because of the following seven measures:
1. General speed limits were introduced (this was the most important measure).
2. It became compulsory to wear a seatbelt, initially in the front seats of passenger cars.
3. It became compulsory for motorcyclists to wear a helmet (it took 10 years for this to be extended to cover moped riders).
4. Road crossings were renovated.
5. A total of 600 km of cycle paths were constructed in urban centres, and action began to separate different forms of traffic into separate lanes.
6. The traffic environment began to be renovated in cities. It was known that the risk of accidents in poorly-

planned urban areas could be up to ten times greater than in wellplanned areas.

7. The renovation of level crossings was accelerated.

Ways of thinking changed. Whereas earlier the blame for traffic accidents was primarily focused on people and their attitudes, and secondly on their vehicle's condition, it was now considered that the main reason was actually the traffic environment itself. A lot of attention was therefore devoted to reforming the traffic environment instead of blaming individual drivers, cyclists or pedestrians.

The debate was extensive and covered matters such as the role of schools, general information campaigns, the poor condition of vehicles, the deterioration of the road network, and tired and drunk drivers.

The public debate was intense and the measures taken started to show results, which added to the enthusiasm. Surprisingly quickly, in the space of about five years, the number of road casualties dropped from 1,200 to around 600, but interest in traffic safety began to wane and numbers started to rise again. It took several years before we came full circle and politicians, the media and citizens once more woke up to the fact that something had to be done.

So original actions were repeated: another Parliamentary Traffic Committee was appointed, several security issues were further discussed, and new and old ideas alike were invented and implemented. It was no surprise that the old truths still applied and the number of casualties fell for a couple of years running. The situation has since stabilised, although the number of cars and the volume of traffic have more than doubled.

Pekka Tarjanne – Minister for trafflc 1972–1975

43 THE NORTH KARELIA PROJECT

Living standards in Finland began to rise rapidly after World War II, and infectious diseases were not having such a big impact on health. In their place had come chronic national diseases, especially heart and vascular disease and cancer. In the 1970s Finland had the highest rate of heart disease in the world. In particular the death of working men due to heart disease was a blow to the health of the nation.

Concerns about the exceptionally high rate of coronary heart disease (CHD) in the Province of North Karelia resulted in a petition being signed in Joensuu in January 1971. Representatives of various groups from the province, led by the governor, appealed to the state authorities for urgent and effective help to improve the alarming situation. And so began the preparatory work which resulted in the launch of the North Karelia Project.

When the project began, cardiovascular disease was already the number one cause of death in the industrialised world, but in the early 1970s much less was known about its causes and the focus had been on treatment and rehabilitation. However, some studies had pointed to some likely causal risk factors, and new information provided new ways to help prevent it. It was observed that there was no reason to blame bacteria or viruses, as with pestilence, but rather that certain lifestyles increased the risk, and it was thus perceived that only preventative measures could bring about any real change in the nation's health. In this way the North Karelia Project set about reducing the nation's risk factors.

The available data showed that the identified risk factors were common among the Finnish and especially the Northern Karelian male population. The population's high serum cholesterol levels could be explained by their diet, which was abundant in saturated fats and salt. It included few vegetables but there was plenty of butter, fat and full-cream milk. It was very common for men to smoke tobacco.

The project's main focus was to change the behaviour of the population (especially smoking and dietary habits), and these starting points created a strategy of community-based prevention work. The goal was to broadly influence the entire community, not just patients in care or those at high risk. In the 1970s this was quite a groundbreaking approach.

Work began with the stated aim of changing the nation's living habits (especially with regards to diet and smoking), but this met with strong opposition in the mainly agrarian community. As the project had a community-based strategy, it did not include centralised intervention, but the work was done through local community organisations and by local people themselves. The project provided the means, trained and motivated the people, and coordinated, monitored and evaluated the activities.

The 5-year project started with a comprehensive baseline study in spring 1972 and ended with a new population survey in spring1977, and the experiences gained there have since been implemented nationally. Preventive measures and monitoring continued in North Karelia until 1997. Over the 25-year period the project achieved all its objectives, and undoubtedly much more.

The published results of the project show how major changes took place with regards to the target risk factors. Male smoking was greatly reduced and dietary habits changed markedly. The changes to the quantity and quality of fat in the diet were especially significant: in 1972 over 80% of the population reported that they mainly used butter on bread, but in 1997 the proportion was less than 10%. Dietary changes have led to about a 17% reduction in the mean serum cholesterol level of the population, and elevated blood pressure has been brought well under control.

Reduced levels of risk factors also led to a rapid decline in mortality rates from coronary diseases. In the 1970s, mortality from CHD among working-age men fell rapidly in North Karelia. National action subsequently led to changes that affected the whole country. The experiences learned from the North Karelia Project have been utilized diversely in e.g. wide-ranging television shows and national projects. It has also shown how modern national diseases could be challenged through lifestyle changes.

The organization that was created to evaluate the North Karelia Project has been developed into the Finnish National Institute for Health and Welfare which carries on monitoring the nation's health. It has demonstrated how the level of risk factors among the Finnish population have fallen very significantly as a result of a drop in smoking and dietary changes. Death from heart disease among working-age men is now 80% lower than when the project began, and death from heart disease has also reduced. Death among working-age men in general has reduced by half and the subjective health of the nation has improved. Finns now enjoy an extra ten years of life expectancy, and they are generally healthy years.

The North Karelia Project has thus become the leading example of how the prevention of heart and vascular disease is possible and worthwhile. While heart diseases and chronic diseases in general have become an important health problem in this day and age, and also the most likely cause of death in the developing countries too (the cause of death in over 60% of all deaths wordwide), the North Karelia Project and Finland's experience are deeply significant. International interest in the results and experiences of the project is very wide. These experiences have been useful in scientific cooperation between different countries and international organizations, especially programmes organized by the WHO.

A top-level UN meeting on the prevention of chronic non-communicable diseases was held in New York in 2011. It was clear that this is not just a national health problem but, especially in developing countries, a future hindrance to social and economic development. The recommendations of the meeting correspond to and also reflect the North Karelia Project and Finland's experiences of it. It is possible to prevent these diseases and essentially improve the health of the nation through influencing people's way of life is the most cost-effective way and a guarantee of future development.

Pekka Puska – Director general, National Public Health Institute

44 SCHIZOPHRENIA PROJECT

In 1980, there were 4.2 psychiatric hospital beds per one thousand inhabitants in Finland; only Ireland had a higher proportion. A couple of years previously, the Finnish Mental Health Act had been reformed with the aim of strengthening outpatient care, but it had had no significant effect. In 1979, what was then the Association of Psychiatric Hospitals filed a motion for the creation of a national programme for schizophrenia treatment. More than half of all psychiatric patients belonged to that diagnosis, and most of them were long-term patients in so-called b-class psychiatric wards, many of which lacked active treatment or rehabilitation programmes.

Based on this motion, in late 1980 the National Board of Health set up a task force to prepare an action plan for schizophrenia research, treatment and rehabilitation. The task force recommended the creation of an active development programme to be implemented in direct interaction with the field. The task force's report, completed in the spring of 1981, formed a basis for just such a project, which was initiated by the National Board of Health, the Hospital Association and the Association of Psychiatric Hospitals. The decision was groundbreaking, as no similar development programme focused on a single illness had ever been implemented in Finland, or in relation to schizophrenia anywhere else in the world.

The National Schizophrenia Project was conducted between 1981 and 1987, with monitoring of its outcomes added in 1992. The quantitative target was to halve the number of new schizophrenia patients and old long-term institutionalised schizophrenia patients in ten years. The most important measure was the development of new, proactive treatment and rehabilitation methods, which were largely focused on families and the living environment. Another objective was the quantitative and qualitative development of outpatient care and its organisers in order to cope with the additional load created by the earlier target. The fulfilment of these targets was monitored with a separate district-specific follow-up study based on patient statistics.

All psychiatric hospital districts participated in the project. Representatives of the hospital districts attended seminars that explained the aims, methods and monitoring of the project. The main approach was to split the project into two extensive sub-projects, one for developing treatments for new schizophrenia patients (usp Project), and another for developing treatments and rehabilitation for long-term patients (psp Project). The development project involved two thirds of Finland's psychiatric hospital districts (14 out of 21).

Previously implemented, new procedures created good conditions for the progress of the main projects. In Turku, Professor Yrjö Alanen and his team had been working on an individual and family-focused psychotherapeutic treatment programme for schizophrenia patients, which suited a public health care system. Alanen was also in charge of the usp Project, so the necessary treatment model was spread around the country. Particularly popular were so-called therapy meetings; meetings where the medical team discussed the initiation of treatment and the patient's care needs with the patient and his/ her family and close relations. The model spread to the other Nordic countries and awakened interest elsewhere. Attention has also been received by the development of long-term patient rehabilitation work by Professor Erik E. Anttinen and his team at the Tampere Sopimusvuori Association. Anttinen was a member of the national development project team, managing the PSP Project. A significant number of long-term patients had already been rehabilitated and released from psychiatric hospitals within the Sopimusvuori Association's therapeutic communities. The project team also set up separate task forces to prepare a report entitled "Schizophrenia and Primary Health Care" and to investigate issues related to preventing illness.

The actions of the National Schizophrenia Project were reported in a total of 15 publications. The end report included well-founded recommendations based on the experiences gained from the development programme, divided into ten areas: prevention, treatment practices, rehabilitation, the care system, qualitative resources, right to basic services, education, development work, research and legislation. A mid-term report published in 1985 indicated that the rehabilitation of long-term patients in particular progressed quickly, even at the early stages of the initiative. It became apparent that hospitals had many fairly moderate schizophrenia cases, which could quickly be rehabilitated into outpatient care. The reduction of new long-term patient cases took more time and often required significant changes in work practices. The project motivated staff and changed the atmosphere in hospitals, when a field that had often felt unrecognised received a new kind of attention.

The project's quantitative targets were well met. According to the follow-up study, the number of new long-term schizophrenia patients fell by 60% and the number of old longterm patients by 67 % between 1982 and 1992. The number of psychiatric hospital beds was reduced by 51% to 1.9 per 1,000 inhabitants. There was also progress in the third objective, i.e. the development of outpatient care: while in 1982 there had been 2.7 outpatient care staff per 10,000 inhabitants, in 1992 there were 5.1. New operating models were developed at a commendable rate, while the number of non-hospital rehabilitation homes, small-scale care homes and assisted living facilities increased. The development trend suffered severe setbacks in the recession of the early 1990s. The number of hospital beds continued to be cut, but outpatient care stopped being increased and was in some cases even reduced. In the twenty-first century the situation has gradually started to normalise.

The schizophrenia project's patient-oriented and humane approach is still present in Finland; in some places strong and under continuous renewal, and in others, weaker. In some areas it runs the risk of being replaced by a more externally focused and excessively medication-oriented approach.

Yrjö Alanen – Professor emeritus of Psychiatry

45 NATIONAL SUICIDE PREVENTION PROJECT

Suicide remains a major public health challenge. Worldwide, one million people take their own lives each year, including over 100,000 in Europe, 60,000 in the EU, and about 4,000 in the Nordic countries. The suicide rate in Finland in 2004 was 20.4 per 100,000.

Finland was the first country to prepare and implement a nationwide suicide prevention strategy – "Suicide can be prevented" – in 1986–96. When the programme was implemented we thoroughly examined every suicide that was committed in Finland in 1987. Researchers spent thousands of hours completing psychological autopsy reports on 1397 suicides, collecting medical, social services and police records, and talking with victims' doctors, nurses, friends, families and employers to help them understand the circumstances surrounding each death. The ambitious programme extended its suicide research and prevention efforts to cover the entire country. It was the first comprehensive effort of its kind anywhere to make a series of recommendations aimed at helping those at greatest risk.

The national programme was implemented in 1992–96 and evaluated by an international peer group in 1996–98. The suicide death rate showed an immediate 15% drop during the implementation period and this downward trend has continued from a peak in 1990 of 30.3 per 100,000 to 20.4 in 2004, a fall of over 30%. This is the level that Finland had about 50 years ago. The comprehensive suicide prevention strategy has successfully reversed the rising suicide trend, which had been climbing from the 1950s until the end of the 1980s.

Despite more and more insight into the pathogenesis of suicidal behaviour, it is currently not sufficiently clear to what extent preventive interventions are linked to its reduction. The need for suicide prevention is obvious, however. The most promising current interventions to prevent suicide are physician education, means restriction and gatekeeper education. Pharmacotherapy, especially with the use of lithium and antidepressants, and to some degree psychotherapy, have also given promising results. Screening programmes have reported some success in identifying individuals with known suicide risk factors, particularly among the school and student population.

Jouko Lönnqvist – Research professor emeritus,
National Institute of Public Health

46 CONTROLLING SEXUALLY TRANSMITTED INFECTIONS

The prevalence of sexually transmitted infections (STI's) in Finland has remained at a reasonable Western European level. In this respect our position is much better than that of our Eastern neighbour, the Russian Federation, where rates of e.g. syphilis and gonorrhoea have been up to a hundred times higher. The Finnish hiv infection rate in 2004 was joint lowest in Europe with Germany, at 24 per million. Other Nordic countries had double the amount of cases, while figures for Russia and Estonia were ten and twenty times higher respectively. In 1990–2001 the total number of HIV infections in Finland among teenagers aged 13–19 was 18. In comparison, Estonia had 748 infected teenagers, and even Sweden had 68. So the statistics show that Finland has been exceptionally successful in the prevention of HIV infections among adults and teenagers alike.

So how has Finland been so successful in preventing STI's and HIV infections? Education has focused on teaching teenagers to take responsibility for their own lives as well as their partners'; mandatory sex education was implemented in comprehensive schools (innovation no. 52) in 1970 and a law was enacted in 1972 which placed family planning counselling services under the jurisdiction of municipal health care centres (innovation no. 38). Schools received public health nurses, who took a leading role in teenage sex education. The use of condoms saw a sharp increase at the end of 1960s, at which time they were used by half of those experiencing sexual intercourse for the first time. Before AIDS became an issue, Finns were the second highest users of condoms in the world, after the Japanese.

Of course there were gaps in sex education and sexual health services in the beginning, but as professionals in the field were trained to higher standards, and attitudes became more liberal, they gradually became areas of more serious professional activity. Follow-up surveys showed a steady increase in sexual knowledge among teenagers and in the use of contraceptives among the general population between the 1970s and 1990s. This led to a comparable decrease in the number of unwanted pregnancies and abortions, and a similar drop in STI's. Instances of gonorrhoea dropped ten-fold during the 1990s. The situation has been helped by the fact that intravenous (IV) drug use has never been as much of a problem in Finland as it has in neighbouring countries. Also, Finland's "harm reduction" approach to IV drug use, an example of which is the free distribution of clean needles, has gathered weight in recent years.

Finland, like its Nordic neighbours, differs from other European countries with regards to the issue of gender equality, which has come so far that moral double standards are already practically non-existent. The empowerment of women has also been positively reflected in the parallel decrease of STI's. Girls use condoms as boldly as boys, and they have learned to exercise their right to safe sexual pleasure (innovation no. 94). The standards expected of a good partner have also risen over the years: he/she is required to be sexually faithful and respond to his/

her partner's sexual desires. This progress has made the prevention of STI's more effective than before.

Only time will tell how much sexual desire will be channelled into the safe, infection-free world of virtual sex, which, as the number of single and partnerless elderly people increases, could turn out to be a true alternative outlet for unfulfilled sexual desire, which people are becoming more unwilling to endure. As a leader in information technology (innovation s nos. 79, 80 and 81), Finland could become a trendsetter for other European countries.

Osmo Kontula – Research professor at the Family Federation of Finland

47 TOBACCO LEGISLATION AND LEGAL ACTIONS

The Finnish strategy to reduce tobacco consumption is based on comprehensive measures, including information campaigns, public health programmes, and protective legislation. The features of this comprehensive policy are a pricing policy, support for stopping smoking, monitoring and research. Continuous monitoring and research play an especially important role.

Awareness of the hazardous effects of tobacco products started to rise at the beginning of the 1960s, when the Parliament (innovation no. 1) unanimously voted for the Government (innovation no. 7) to take immediate action on reducing the negative effects of smoking. This was an important step, but legislation on reducing tobacco consumption was only passed 15 years later, in 1976.

The most progressive Tobacco Act of its time prohibited all forms of tobacco advertising, introduced compulsory health warnings on tobacco packages, prohibited the sale of tobacco products to persons evidently under 16 years of age and prohibited smoking at school, (partially) on public transport and in most indoor public venues.

When indications on the negative health effects of environmental tobacco smoke were confirmed in the 1980s, the Finnish Parliament started to formulate new tobacco legislation in order to prevent public exposure.

In 1995 the law was amended to prohibit smoking in workplaces, with bars and restaurants as the only exception. These too became smoke-free in June 2007. The law provided, however, for a two-year transition period, so the final deadline for all bars and restaurants to be smoke-free was June 2009. According to the Tobacco Act, smoking is forbidden in all catering establishments irrespective of their size or the type of license they have. Pubs and restaurants may build separate smoking booths but the smoke must not enter the smoke-free area. The smoking booth is intended to be a place that people use quickly and leave. The area is intended purely for smoking: it is not allowed to serve or consume food or drink there or have any gaming machines etc. The smoking booth is not a licensed area.

The prohibition of smoking in the living environment is especially aimed at protecting children. The indoor premises of children's private daycare as well as both the indoor and outdoor areas of public daycare centres must be smoke-free. In addition, institutions that provide care for persons under the age of 18 must be totally smoke free (inside and outside).

Smoking is not allowed in the indoor premises of educational institutions that provide basic, vocational or upper secondary education or in their student dormitories, and neither is it allowed in outdoor areas in their use.

The indoor areas of government agencies and authorities and comparable public bodies intended for the public and clients are also smoke-free. Public transport is also smoke-free.

The prohinbition of smoking in workplaces, public events and residential buildings are to ensure that nobody is unwillingly exposed to tobacco smoke. Smoking is not allowed in the joint facilities of apartment houses or housing communities, indoor public events and hotel rooms. Hotels can reserve one out of ten rooms for smokers.

Shelters and spectators' halls outside, for example the front stage and the immediate vicinity accessible to the audience, must be smoke-free. The organizers of outdoor public events have to indicate the section where smoking is allowed.

Finland was the first country in the world to classify environmental tobacco smoke as a carcinogenic substance by law in July 2000.

The EU tobacco advertising directive came into force on 31.7.2005 forbidding tobacco advertising in printed media, radio and the Internet. The directive also placed limits on tobacco companies' sponsorship of cultural and sporting events. Local events which involve participants from only one member state are not covered by this directive. Finland has implemented the directive as part of the legal system.

Finland has also limited the advertising of tobacco products: since the beginning of July 2009 travelers have only been allowed to bring 200 cigarettes, 50 cigars, 100 cigarillos and 250 grammes of pipe or rolling tobacco into the country if the foreign-bought produce does not have Finnish and Swedish warning labels on them.

The sale of tobacco products is licensed and granting and monitoring must be paid for. A small sales license for tobacco is granted by the municipality, and costs 50–200 euros depending on the number of sales points. There is also an inspection fee, which costs 50–100 euros per point of sale. The license may be withdrawn if illegal sales continue after an official warning. This is to encourage sellers to monitor themselves and to prevent the sale of tobacco to minors. A license is also required to buy tobacco from a wholesaler. The licensing system has signigicantly decreased the number of points of sales.

The smallest packages that tobacco may be sold in is 20 cigarettes, 10 cigarillos and 30 grammes of loose tobacco.

The stated aim of the 2010 tobacco law is to stop the use of products that are harmful to people's health and which cause dependence.

The tobacco law forbids

1) The display of tobacco products in retail stores (not including tobacco shops where the products cannot be seen from the outside)
2) The delivery, import or storing of tobacco by anyone under 18 years old
3) The sale of tobacco in e.g. daycares, schools and educational institutions and their environment
4) The import, sale or other distribution of oral tobacco products (up to 30 boxes containing 30 grams of snuff and a maximum of 200 cigarettes, more if they have been labeled with the appropriate health warnings in Finnish and Swedish) may be imported for personal use)
5) The sale of tobacco products from vending machines (from 2015)
6) Tobacco sponsorship

A seller of tobacco must be at least 18 years old, smokeless areas will increase to include areas used by children and youths, areas shared by different inhabitants of a building, outdoor events and hotels.

Nicotine replacement products may be sold from pharmacies and retail stores, kiosks, petrol stations and restaurants that have a tobacco license.

The objective of the Finnish Tobacco Act (2010) is to put an end to the use of tobacco products in Finland by 2040. This means that the use of tobacco products will no longer be a permanent feature of society and people's lives, and that society is willing to support this effort.

The smoke-free Finland 2040 network is to support the objective of out Tobacco Act. The network will urge and support the Finnish government to undertake policies that will make Finland smoke-free by 2040.

The first European legal case against the tobacco companies began in Finland in 1988. The plaintiff was pensioner Pentti Aho, who started smoking in 1941 at the age of 16. He became ill with smoking-induced chronic bronchitis and emphysema in 1980 and laryngeal cancer in 1986, and he died in 1992.

The product liability suit against Oy Rettig Ab and Suomen Tupakka – BAT Nordic Oy was based on the right to receive compensation because the companies had manufactured and sold a product that is hazardous to human health against a legal prohibition. The companies had also concealed the health hazards caused by their products, prevented outsiders from warning their clients, and had actively lied to consumers when they stated that cigarettes do not harm health.

The Finnish product liability case was dismissed by the City Court and the Court of Appeal, and the Supreme Court were also of the same opinion. The Supreme Court also removed the tobacco companies' obligation to issue warnings.

Legal actions against Philip Morris and British American Tobacco were filed in March 2005. In this case, which focuses on light cigarettes, the plaintiffs claim that Amer Oy (which no longer exists) and Suomen Tupakka – BAT

Nordic Oy (which no longer has production facilities in Finland) had aimed to create addiction by manufacturing cigarettes and have, without exception, denied and concealed the fact that their products might cause addiction in their marketing since the 1950s. In October 2008 Helsinki City Court dismissed the case, and so did the Court of Appeal in 2010. The appeal to the Supreme Court was withdrawn, so the decision is now final.

Mervi Hara – Executive director, Finland's ASH

48 XYLITOL

Finnish dental researchers started to take an interest in xylitol at the beginning of the 1970s, at which time the first research project on xylitol's effect on dental plaque was conducted in the Faculty of Dentistry in the University of Turku. The final clinical results of the research were published in 1975, and in the same year the predecessor of all health-improving food products, the world's first xylitol-sweetened confection, Xylitol-Jenkki chewing gum, was launched. Since that time several comprehensive clinical dental studies have been conducted on xylitol, both in Finland and abroad.

Xylitol is a natural sweetener that is most highly concentrated in plums, strawberries, cauliflower and raspberries. Even the human body produces xylitol, approximately 5 to 15 grammes per day. Industrially, xylitol can be produced from e.g. the birch fibre xylane.

Xylitol's teeth-friendly effects are based on the fact that bacteria which causes caries cannot effectively feed on xylitol, and a regular intake can also diminish the quantity of harmful bacteria in the mouth and make it easier to brush away. Xylitol immediately neutralises harmful acids.

A mother-child research project in the University of Turku at the beginning of the 1990s showed that the mother's regular consumption of xylitol chewing gum decreased the motherchild transmission of caries bacteria and reduced dental decay in milk teeth by 70%.

Research on xylitol is now also conducted in other fields of medicine; a study in the Department of Paediatrics in the University of Oulu showed that chewing xylitol gum can significantly reduce the number of ear infections in children, and it also has a beneficial effect on the quality and quantity of saliva, making it useful in the treatment of dry mouth.

It is important that dental care is seen as a worthwhile, pleasant and simple part of life, and the power of xylitol lies in the fact that it offers a good-tasting and pleasant way of cultivating a healthy mouth. Taking care of oral hygiene, using fluoride toothpaste, healthy and regular dining habits and xylitol chewing gum and sweets are all excellent ways of maintaining oral health.

Marjatta Sandström – Former Spokesperson
for xylitol for Leaf Suomi Ltd.

CULTURE

49 THE FINNISH LITERATURE SOCIETY

Elias Lönnrot wrote in the minutes of the Finnish Literature Society's inaugural meeting on 16 February 1831 that "during their meeting they began to speak of Finnish books, and the Finnish language, and how best they could serve literary requirements. The evening concluded that, all in all, it is easier to work together than alone, so we discussed the need to form a Society..." This practical aim was soon transformed into a means of implementing the ideals of the Finnish national consciousness.

The Enlightenment, Romanticism and Nationalism were all sources of inspiration for the creation of the grand Fennomanian project, which involved reforming the Finnish language, creating literature, documenting folklore, writing a history and constructing a Finnish national identity. The project was put into effect at the Finnish Literature Society through the invention of neologisms, large dictionary projects, the collection of folklore, literature prizes, and the publication of the *Kalevala* and *Kanteletar*, historical works, and plays and novels. In short, the Society played a critical role in creating opportunities for scholarly activity and popular education in modern Finland, without which the country would never have become the modern industrial state and civic society that it is today. The reforms thus engendered a society that aimed to guarantee all its members the opportunity to gain access to scholarly information and culture – as well as political influence.

The work of the Finnish Literature Society resulted in the creation, documentation and dissemination of knowledge and culture that had traditionally been based on memory; the spoken word assumed a literary form. This change resulted in society becoming literate, which did not just affect the dissemination and documentation of information but equally its creation and the conceptualisation of reality.

During the 19th century the Society spawned all the major scholarly Finnish language societies and many institutions, and it played a role in the birth of the National Theatre, Finnish national business life and capital, and the creation of the party system. Although the Society moved in 1890 into its fine residence in the capital and was run by an elite group of gentlemen from Helsinki, it created an axis that permeated Finnish society and culture and was balanced at the other end by local masters of folklore.

The Society has changed over the years from being a nation builder to a scholarly deposit of memories. During its over 180 years in existence it has enhanced Finnish self-understanding, promoted an awareness of Finnish literature in Finland and abroad and published a significant tranche of Finnish fiction, non-fiction and scholarly literature. As a cultural organisation, language and identity have served as the ideological stimuli for the Society's activities, but researching the building blocks of language and identity has also been of key importance – together with a critical examination of the ideals, traditions and historical phenomena that support these two concepts.

The aim of the Finnish Literature Society has been and continues to be to make Finnish culture understandable to ourselves as Finns and others.

Tuomas M. S. Lehtonen – Secretary general,
Finnish Literature Society

50 THE FINNO-UGRIAN SOCIETY

In the beginning, before the concept of Finnishness existed, there was Finno-Ugrianism. It was known that the Finnish language was unrelated to Hebrew or Greek, the language of antiquity and the Bible. It was assumed that languages that were spoken in northern Eurasia and the people who lived there would be able to reveal undocumented history from the ancient past, so passionate information-seekers and courageous travelers were required and their mission lasted several generations.

The Finno-Ugrian Society was founded in 1883 to promote the study of the language, culture and history of the Ugric and Altaic people. Dozens of scholarships have been awarded over the years to enable the collection of a wealth of material on Finno-Ugrianism from around the Ural mountains and the so-called Altaic languages from the land that lies between the Atlantic and the Pacific Oceans. The society has published hundreds of books, reports, analyses and collections of material. This mass of information means that Finno-Ugrianism has been mapped far more concretely than was the case when the society was founded, but in fact new studies are still being produced, and no final answer has yet been produced to the question of Finno-Ugrianism. The ongoing question is still two the languages are related and how many thousand years are needed to explain the diversity between them.

The area under study has from the very beginning been understood to be the areas where Uralic and Altaic languages are spoken, which consists of dozens of different kinds of ethnic communities who had several different ways of interpreting the mundane and the sacred. When large-scale field trips were undertaken, Finno-Ugric communities generally used the same language they had inherited from their ancestors, and their culture had been handed down in the same fashion as they in turn passed their legacy to their descendants. This was interrupted however by the Russian revolution, Stalin's purges, the Second World War and urbanization. Scandinavian Sámi people, Mordvin, Cheremis (Mari), Votjak (Urdmurt), Ostyak (Khanty) and Vogul (Mantsy) and different kinds of Samoyedic populations all received a researcher, aided by a scholarship, from the Finno-Ugrian Society, as did Mongols who spoke Altaic languages.

Heikki Paasonen's Mordvin material and Artturi Kannisto's Mantsy collections were edited over the next 100 years until they were ready for publication. G.J. Ramstedt, who studied Mongols, was the unluckiest of the large group who received a scholarship from the society: his first large collection of material was stolen. He returned to Finland almost empty-handed but he pulled himself together and returned to the field, going even further east, as far as Japan and Korea. Ramstedt wrote the first and for a long time the only English-language book on the Korean language which was published in 1939. When the Korean War began, the U.S. Army bought the entire stock.

The most famous recipient of the stipend was C.G. Mannerheim, who made his famous trip, which was also designed to enable the collection of military intelligence, in 1906–08. To disguise the true reason for his trip, he collected a lot of valuable ethnographic material and above all photographed life in western and northern China, traveling by horse through all the four seasons. Mannerheim's photographic negatives have survived in good nough condition to be converted into digital form, and they are highly valued in modern-day China for their authenticity.

Many of the Finno-Ugrian Society researchers who were granted scholarships at the end of the 19th century and beginning of the 20th century predicted perceived an ongoing change in language and predicted that the language would die and be superseded in most cases by Russian. In many cases this has come to pass and Finno-Ugricness in the 21st century is characterized by old, autochthonous linguistic societies' minority status, and linguistic rights are usually lacking or completely absent. The dictionaries that the society released on the Liv and Kamasin languages in 1938 and 1944 respectively are already the most important documents on dead languages. Subsequent dictionaries on Khanty (1948), Skolt and Skolt Lappish (1958), Carelian (1968–2005) and Mordvin (1990–1999) are classics in their genre and important sources of the respective languages, together with the other materials that were collected. The Finnish etymological dictionary was also published by the society in 1955–1981.

The Finno-Ugrian Society is still one of the more important international publishers of research in the field, and it also serves as a place for researchers to gather. Many Finno-Ugrian communities that speak minority languages that aim to develop and research their language have found the society's publications to be a rich source for their cultural inheritance. The strongest tradition is still the holding of the A.G.M. on the discipline founder M.A. Castren's birthday on December 2. This has lasted since 1884.

Let us then here at the end of the article reveal the truth about the Finno-Ugric linguistic family: it was already perceived by Hungarian researchers in the 18th century. The Finno-Ugric llinguistic family is nowadays known quite well, but many languages are in worse straits than ever. The research community's mission continues.

Riho Grünthal – Professor in Helsinki University
Department of Finno-Ugrian studies

51 FINNISH LIBRARIES

Finns are world-record library users: The average Finn borrows more than 20 books per year, and visits the library around once a month. But why do we use libraries so eagerly?

Libraries have become part of life in Finland. Knowledge per se is appreciated; quizzes are popular and encyclopaedias sell in record numbers.

Libraries are popular because they answer people's individual needs. Schools and the mass media deliver ready-made chunks of information and life experience, but the library system is better tuned in to answering individual questions. The more demanding the question, the surer you can be that the library will be better able to help than search engines like Google.

Today, every municipality (innovation no. 4) in Finland has a public library. They have grown to function far beyond the limits of a "book circulation centre", lending music and videos and offering access to computers. They analyse information content systematically using qualitative criteria. They help learners, active citizens and everybody else to find the information they are looking for, and they also organise storytelling circles, art exhibitions and film presentations.

Finnish public libraries are free of charge, and citizens have equal access to knowledge and culture in every part of the country, which is part of the reason that Finland does so well in international PISA learning studies (innovation no. 54).

The strength of the Finnish public library system has several sources, not least the large contribution that the state has made over the decades – up until the 1990s Finnish public libraries were less dependent on local budgets than libraries in many other countries. Library professionals are highly educated, and every Finnish library is part of a national network – if one library doesn't have a certain item it can be ordered from another, be it a research or public library. The sharing of resources demands a lot of cooperation and coordination, which is nowadays mainly achieved via the Internet.

The basic idea of the Finnish library strategy is a sensible division of labour between local, regional and national levels, allowing each level to concentrate on the work that is most relevant to it. For example, a local library can focus on direct customer service because resources which are produced on national and regional levels are accessible via the Internet. The best example of this is the brand new information search portal "Tiedonhaun Portti", which is based on the concept of the Semantic Web and combines existing library and Internet resources in a revolutionary way. It has the same ideology as the Linux (innovation no. 81) community. Nowadays libraries also make use of Facebook and Twitter.

From a wider social perspective the Information Society should activate a person's creative capacity, and easy access to information and culture is required to promote inclusion and integration. The library system is a high quality, user-oriented tool which furthers both aims, so it is part of the Finnish Government Programme. It is accepted as a fact that funding libraries means funding democracy and development.

Kaarina Dromberg – Minister of culture 2002–2003

52 FINNISH COMPREHENSIVE SCHOOLS

Education planners dreamed of a comprehensive basic school system for more than a century before the preconditions required by such a venture began to be fulfilled in the 1960s, when agrarian Finland began a course of rapid industrialisation. Companies had to be able to compete on an international level and the manufacturing of quality products required a well-educated labour force, while the concurrent goal of the construction of a Nordic welfare society demanded a highly educated labour force to work in the public sector. The service sector expanded so quickly that people started talking about a service society as well as an industrial one. This dynamic development required that all possible reserves of talent be put to good use.

Apart from the economic factors, social equality rose to become a central political goal. In the middle of the 1960s the Centre Party supported the left wing, forming the necessary political power base (innovation no. 7) to create a comprehensive school system for basic education, and in 1968 the Finnish Parliament (innovation no. 1) accepted a law which guaranteed every child and youth a high-standard basic nine-year education irrespective of where they lived or the wealth of their parents. The essential thing was that, when the law was prepared, a good basic education was seen as an essential human right, which meant that intellectually and developmentally disabled children also had the right to grow and develop. The comprehensive school really became a school for all.

The reform of the education system required a corresponding reform of teacher education, so they were carried out at the same time. The education of teachers was transferred to the universities (innovation no. 53), where they would study to masters degree level. In order to guarantee the availability of highly educated teachers in the peripheral areas, courses began in seven universities around the country including Northern and Eastern Finland.

Responsibility for the implementation and ongoing development of basic education lies squarely with the municipalities. This structure underlines the essential role of education as a basic service, with all decisions being made at ground level. The relationship between municipal autonomy (innovation no. 4) and national education goes back more than a century. In Finland there are over 300 municipalities, which means that the local school administration involves thousands of pupils' parents. The comprehensive school is thus part of Finnish democracy, part of the implementation of the subsidiary principle.

The development of comprehensive schools has been a long process, and shows that education is always closely related to the society's political, cultural and economic development. The success of Finnish pupils in international comparisons is the sum of various factors (innovation no. 54).

The integrated comprehensive school is an excellent Finnish innovation. In a society with a tendency towards polarisation it is even more important as a factor that unites the nation. It strengthens national identity but also encourages international and intercultural interaction.

At the moment, the comprehensive school is the flagship of our first-class educational system. It offers a good basis for providing quality education in vocational and secondary schools, and is always being developed to keep it relevant in an ever-changing political, cultural and economic environment. As professor Kari Uusikylä said, a good school must be constructed every day from scratch.

Erkki Aho – General director, Finnish national board of education, 1973–1991

53 FREE EDUCATION

Finnish education has a good reputation around the world. Its characteristic features are:
- free education
- every child and youth has a right and duty to study and learn
- it is based on a national curriculum
- regional educational administration
- strong trust in teachers' abilities
- possibilities for flexible study paths
- high levels of academic achievement across the country

The system's cornerstone is the fact that education is routinely provided for all children and youths who reside in Finland, irrespective of their nationality, gender or social, economic or cultural background. Administration of the education system has been devolved to regional level, but every school adheres to the national curriculum. This guarantees quality education across the whole country in every town and village, irrespective of any special local features. There are no national tests upon completing the basic education, and schools are not publicly graded. Teachers rely on national guidelines when they evaluate the pupils at the end of their basic education. The application and evaluation processes are transparent, equal and independent of where the applicant was educated because the grounds for the evaluations are clear and explicit across the whole country.

The Finnish education system doesn't have any educational dead-ends or institutionalized paths. Any student can apply for any level of further education irrespective of where they completed their basic aducation and be accepted as a student if they pass. Education is free. Competition for study places is decided on merit, not relationships or money or earlier choices.

The Finnish comprehensive school system provides a very good education, and 15-year-old students who have completed their studies consistently score remarkably high results in international comparisons across the board, in mother-tongue studies, mathematics and the sciences. After the basic schooling finishes, further education is available and recommended to everyone. Around 92% (in 2009) of students progress to high school and polythechnics, which prepares them to enter higher education at home and abroad. Those who do not continue with school are provided with free educational alternatives.

Vocational education in Finland is a high-quality and free way to learn a trade. It offers college-based training as well as external placements and gives the students the skill they need to make the transition to working life when they complete their studies. Vocational education is just as popular as high school, and many of those who complete the second phase find a job right away, while others continue to the higher level or transfer to university.

High school education is chosen by around half of those who have finished their basic studies, and at its completion pupils take part in national tests. High school education is free. Studies can take 2–4 years, depending on the pace the student goes at. The student's education is comprised of subjects dictated by the national curriculum supplemented by courses that can be freely chosen.

After the second phase of education has been completed in high school or vocational education, the student can apply to progress to university or polythechnic, where a test must be passed to gain entry. Education is free and when it is successfully completed the student is awarded a university or polytechnic degree. A successful applicant has the right to strive to complete a bachelor's or master's degree without having to take any more tests. The studies and graduation are free, which is an important factor in attracting foreign students to study in Finland. The fact that education can be both free and of a high standard is a cause for wonder in many international discussions.

The basic concept is that all students who are equally talented and hardworking should receive the same kind of support and be offered the possibility to continue their studies free of charge. Youths can get professional supervision to plan their future studies an learn about the different options. The student grant system provides financial support and the fact that even higher educationis free is a sign of equality and justice with regards to education.

Sonja Kosunen – Former parliamentary assistant of minister of education

54 LITERACY OF FINNISH CHILDREN

In recent years it seems like a new international sport has been invented: evaluating educational achievement. In particular the Orgnisation for Economic Co-operation and Development OECD has been interested in the area and has organized tests in literacy, mathematics and the natural sciences which are known as the Programme for International Stu-dent Assessment (PISA) studies. They consider the test results of 15-year-old pupils in over 30 countries.

Finnish students have done well in all of the PISA studies, and the results for literacy in particular have been noticed internationally. This has let to researchers and teachers from all over the world coming to Finland to get to know the Finnish education system and how it is implemented. Furthermore, Finnish experts are invited all over thre world to lecture on education politics. Everyone has the same burning question: what is the high rate of Finnish literacy based on?

This simple question has no simple answer. Good results are often the sum of various factors: The structure of the educational system (the whole age-group has been schooled for 9 years), local decision-making authority and didactic autonomy, pupil-centred teaching, special remedial teaching that has been developed over a long period of time for students with learning difficulties, student care and other practices that support teaching (education counselling, school psychologists, school social workers, school health services), teachers with a sense of vocation, free education.

Facts about the school system alone cannot explain the good results however; the conditions of society at large must also be taken into account. Two of the most important factors that support the high rate of literacy in Finland are a culture that supports reading and a long tradion of it too. Over the centuries the Church has been responsible for Finns' literacy. The protestant religion's principle that everyone should be able to read the Bible and other religious books meant firstly that it was necessary to have books in Finnish and secondly that people had to become literate. It is no coincidence that the first book ever published in Finnish was an ABC book in the middle of the 16th century.

The literacy of the people was considerably influenced by a decree in the 1660s that made literacy a prerequisite of marriage. The Church employed schoolmasters to teach the people and the parish clerk's duties included organising reading classes and recitals, and parents were also dutybound to teach their children at home. The Church was authoritarian in nature at this time. It is important to underline just how egalitarian the literacy efforts were. Since the beginning it has been carefully guaranteed that the basics of literacy are taught to all citizens, regardless of their status or position in society. This was not an easy task as children were at very different stages in terms of readiness to learn, and early teachers had not had any kind of pedagogic training to prepare them for learning difficulties. But they dug deep and succeeded. Literacy began to be regarded as a necessary skill for every adult even before oraganised national education existed. Social pressure supported the acquisition of literacy before any rules or regulations were in place. There were deficiencies and areas of concern in the teaching, however, and this led to the development of new methods.

Finnish nationalism began to be stirred up in the 19th century with the help of language and literature. There was a desire to purposefully civilise Finns and this required new educational institutions, literature in the mothertongue, youth groups and labour movements. Literature leaned heavily towards depicting the lives of ordinary people, which in itself rooted a positive attitude towards literacy in the national psyche.

Finns are avid readers of books and newspapers, and Finnish homes contain significantly more books on average than other European homes. They also have one of the highesdt newspaper readership rates in the world. Finnish children are used to magazines being orderd to the house (they are delivered to the home, which is unusual in an international context), and family life usually includes reading. Every home has at least a few books, and a bookshelf is standard furniture. In accordance with all this, books are often given as gifts at Christmas and for birthdays and graduations. Both studies and practical observations point to the fact that the more books there are in the house, the more children will use them.

Finland has a uniquely comprehensive library system which includes mobile library vans, both in the city and the countryside. This gives rise to a chicken-and-egg conundrum: when books are available, books will also be requested, and when people request books then in a democratic country they will be available.

Jukka Sarjala – Genera director, Finnish national board of education, 1995–2002

55 UNIVERSITY DECENTRALISATION

Until the 1920s Finnish university education was restricted to Helsinki, and even at the end of the 1950s it was largely centred in the capital. There was the University of Helsinki, with a full range of disciplines, the Helsinki University of Technology and the Helsinki School of Economics and Business Administration, as well as the Swedish School of Economics and Business Administration, the University of Social Sciences and the College of Veterinary Medicine. Art and music academies were also developing.

In the city of Turku the Swedish-language (innovation no. 11) Turku Academy started teaching in 1919, the Finnish-language University of Turku in 1922. At the end of the 1950s almost all Finnish university students studied in Helsinki.

Intensive development of the Finnish university system began in the 1960s, when the Higher Education Development Act, which was initiated by President Urho Kekkonen and a broad-based coalition government (innovation no. 7), was passed, providing universities with the guarantee of gradually increasing resources, creating a comprehensive system for student financial aid (innovation no. 56), and decentralising higher education throughout Finland by creating several new university units.

The University of Oulu opened its doors in autumn 1959, Jyväskylä's traditional Teacher Training Centre was gradually turned into a university, and in February and

March of 1966 Acts were passed regarding the founding of universities in Kuopio and Joensuu and universities of technology in Lappeenranta and Tampere. Academic education also became available in Vaasa through a governmental decision. The new system was complemented by the University of Lapland in Rovaniemi, which started teaching in autumn 1979, and some universities have created satellite units in nearby towns. One result of these developments is that, at the beginning of the 21st century, the majority of Finnish university students study outside the capital.

The decentralisation of Finland's university education system has probably been the fastest and most sweeping in the whole of Europe, but it has been successful in many ways.

Decentralised university education has guaranteed Finns an equal opportunity to study at a higher level irrespective of where they live, which makes it easier for universities to find and utilise the reserves of talent that the country has at its disposal. Similar developments were carried out concerning music education in the post-war period; the creation of a wide and comprehensive network of music education institutions (innovation no. 57) is probably an important factor in Finland's international success in the field.

A geographically diverse university system has delivered a highly capable academic labour force in almost all fields all over the country. The success and growth of the new university cities of Oulu, Jyväskylä, Vaasa, Kuopio, Joensuu and Lappeenranta is above all down to their universities, without which these old urban centres would probably have stagnated and decayed.

The decentralised university system also enables the

creation of wide and functional international connections in the fields of science and education. If universities only existed on the south coast of the country it would be difficult for them to maintain lively and innovative contacts with universities in e.g. Tromsø and Umeå in Northern Scandinavia; Petrozavodsk, Archangel and Syktyvkar in Northern Russia; or even St. Petersburg and the northernmost parts of the American continent. Lively contacts with the wide university system in central Europe also require several actors.

In addition, the European Union emphasises direct contact between different European regions, and the universities in different regions of Finland contribute to making these encounters possible and useful.

Recent comments regarding the fragmented nature of Finnish university education are based on the overemphasis of certain narrow industrial and production requirements, and are incorrect from the point of view of Finland's national interests as a whole and the broad-based education of the whole population. These critics seem to have forgotten that it was precisely this university education system (innovation no. 53) that produced Finland's high-level educational system and high standards of technical education. In fact the Finnish university system, which has modern buildings and is often well-equipped, offers – given enough resources and sufficient internal networks and connections with the Finnish economic sphere – good conditions to create new innovations, increase interdisciplinary and international connections, and welcome plenty students from other parts of the world.

Jaakko Numminen – Minister, permanent secretary of the Ministry of Education 1973–1994

56 STUDENT GRANTS

The history of Finnish student grants dates back to 1969 when an Act was passed, according to which the state would act as guarantor for student loans, and in 1972 students were also provided, in addition to the student loan, with a study grant. At that time the study grant was quite small compared to the student loan though, so students were obliged to take the loan. In the middle of the 1970's, however, the increasing amount of student loans resulted in banks refusing to grant them. After some debate the amount of student loan was reduced (in 1977), and this loss was compensated by housing benefit, which was intended to cover only housing costs, and subsidised meals for higher education students, which were introduced in 1979 when President Kekkonen discovered that more than half of higher education students were in worse physical shape than he was. Subsidised interest on student loans was introduced in 1983, because support for their repayment was also considered important. The student loan was the so-called "excess clause" of the sum total of investing in a university education. Even if the investment did not produce the desired result, i.e. a job, the Finnish State wanted to support the repayment of the student loan.

In 1992 a big reform of student financial aid was implemented, increasing the proportional amount of study grant in relation to the study loan and making it liable to taxation. At the same time subsidised interest loans were replaced by commercial student loans. The income and wealth of the higher education student's parents and spouse were no longer taken into account in decisions on study grants, and a maximum eligibility period was introduced. In 1994 a similar reform was carried out on non-university student financial aid. More recently the maximum rent level of the housing supplement was raised and the student loan was made tax-deductible.

Student financial aid is subject to the fulfilment of eligibility criteria and results. This means that the student is not eligible for financial aid if their studies are not progressing sufficiently well. In addition, student financial aid must be repaid if the student has received sufficient income from other sources. Student financial aid is intended as the main way for students to finance their studies, rather than a supplement to other income. Student financial aid is not intended to make people rich but rather guarantee everyone's right to study and get a profession. The total student financial aid paid is around 2% of Finland's gross national product, which means that it has plenty of advocates and critics. Some think that the 2% is justified if we aim to maintain the competitivity of Finnish society, but it is a lot of money for a small country. It is however crucial to ensure that everyone has the possibility to study. A country with little more than 5 million inhabitants cannot afford to lose its best components, so in this way student financial aid is justified. Student financial aid has provided a stable tax income and thus also benefited the welfare state. Finland's competitivity is based on high quality education, an equal educational system and an educated labour force.

Elina Karjalainen – National Union of Students in Finland, member of the secretariat 2002–2005

57 MUSIC SCHOOLS

We Finns have always been crazy about music. It is our number one hobby, providing resources and preconditions for a good everyday life. Almost one hundred music schools have been founded in Finland over the decades, a network which is unique on a global scale. Thanks to the schools' creative work, Finland's musical life is internationally esteemed.

The State has supported this creativity by means of extracurricular art education for children and youths. It is target-oriented education with ascending levels which provides students with a means of self-expression and prepares them for vocational training or higher education in the field. This extra-curricular art education is not a substitute for art education in comprehensive schools, but it gives pupils the opportunity to deepen their skills and knowledge. Over 10% of Finland's comprehensive school students participate in extra-curricular art education. Most of them, over 60,000 children and adolescents, study in music schools, which are subsidised by the State to the tune of 47 million euros. The objective of music education is not only to produce professionals – the ability to participate in art education and artistic life is seen as a fundamental right and a way to promote creativity and boost self-esteem.

We Finns are melancholy by nature, and we have traditionally let loose by singing and playing. Sing-songs have always been popular, and many Finns currently have a karaoke machine at home. Music is the most sociable art form and it has had a deep effect on us. It is well known in Finland that new kinds of thoughts cannot arise without creativity and strong self-esteem.

Human capital cannot accrue without constant cultural and artistic inspiration. Culture is a central societal resource, and art starts with children and adolescents. Fortunately, efforts have been made to realise this principle during recent years. However, it must be admitted that we Finns are still at an early stage on our cultural journey and the zenith of our creativity may be decades away. Music schools have been the driving force of the Finnish nation, and we must make sure that they carry us into the future.

Minna Lintonen – Member of Parliament 2003–2007

58 NON-FORMAL ADULT EDUCATION

Nordic popular and adult education movements were based on the ideals of lifelong learning and active and responsible citizenship long before these factors were regulated by law in the Act on Liberal Adult Education. The Danish folk high school movement sees its educational tasks from three perspectives: philosophical, political and practical. The folk high school – the school of life and the living word – is for education, not for learning by rote contents decreed by others. Thus the philosophical basis of popular education lies in respect for human worth and for the individual's ability to understand their own needs for education. Popular education is political in that enlightenment is at the root of democracy. An enlightened citizen can influence the issues that affect her life and feel responsible for fellow citizens.

As a result of the changing society, the objective of "popular enlightenment" has shifted from forming a national identity to educating responsible citizens. Currently, the main objectives of popular education in the Nordic countries are to promote multicultural and diverse interaction between different ethnic groups and to strengthen the identity and citizenship of immigrants. The joint educational mission is now global citizenship.

European debates on the opportunities of lifelong learning have drawn attention to recognising the importance of everyday learning. The Nordic style of institutionalised non-formal adult education based on the society's desire for education and maintained by communities has not always fitted seamlessly into the pan-European concept of "everyday learning", despite the fact that its educational and work methods are familiar in their many variations to most European countries.

Finland has also conducted debates as to whether the historical institutional structure of its non-formal adult education is a condition or an obstacle to the adult education needs of today's society. In evaluating the institutional structure and mission of non-formal adult education it should be remembered that our popular education efforts are based on the citizens' desire for education, and are established and maintained by popular movements. Cooperation between different operating models can and should of course be promoted, but institutions cannot and should not be closed down unless those who run them decide to do so.

The Liberal Adult Education Act was compiled to cover a nationwide network of institutions, of which there are now approximately 330: adult education centres (of which there are currently some 200), folk high schools (88), study centres (11), sports institutes (11) and summer universities (20). Their educational services are currently used by more than one million citizens annually, a figure which is unsurpassed anywhere in the world.

Adult education centres are mainly municipally owned. The number of adult education centres doubled in the 1960s, peaking at nearly 280. Even today, the centres' services cover all Finnish municipalities. Naturally, their operations vary greatly. These kinds of municipal educational institutions based on the citizens' own needs are unique in the world.

The Act on Liberal Adult Education defines folk high schools as boarding schools that may in their work emphasise their own values, ideological backgrounds and educational objectives. Already in the 1890s, Finland's university students' associations set up 16 Finnish-language and six Swedish-language folk high schools, reflecting provincial and national wishes for education. On Finland's independence in 1917, there were 36 folk high schools, of which two were based on Christian ideology. In the following decades various revivalist and ecclesiastical movements set up a network of Christian institutes in Finland, and in the 1920s they were joined by the workers' movement's and the youth association movement's own institutions.

The folk high school movement is Finland's largest private educational network, and the institutes' operators provide an unusually comprehensive representation of the diversity of Finnish society.

The task of organisational study centres is to promote the fulfilment of equality and diversity in Finnish society. Study centres exist mainly to meet the educational needs of their member organisations. The basic principles of their operations are shared participation, self-directedness and dialogue. As organisations, they are flexible, operating wherever the learners are. The biggest single subject of teaching at study centres is civic and organisational activities. Some study centres offer adult education and sociocultural activities to non-members, but not to the same extent as for instance in Sweden, where up to 20% of the population participates in study groups annually.

In Finland there are more than 250,000 annual participants in study centres' educational activities.

Finland's sports institutes were also set up by popular and, in some cases, ideological movements. The Varala Institute was established in Tampere as early as 1909 by female gymnasts. Sports institutes first received recognition as their own category of educational institution in 1961.

The birth of the summer university institution was also linked to provincial educational aspirations and the building of a national identity. The first summer university association was established in Jyväskylä in 1912. Most other summer universities were established in the 1950s and 60s, mainly by action of provincial university networks. Currently, summer universities operate in 140 districts around Finland.

Thus, all forms of non-formal adult education in Finland spring from the desire for education of the society. The core function of non-formal and liberal adult education is to strengthen the civic society and to facilitate equitable participation, as defined in the mission of the Parliamentary Adult Education and Training Committee.

Jyrki Ijäs – Secretary general, Finnish folk high school association

59 FIGURENOTE METHOD

What should you do if you want to start to play an instrument but you don't read music? One cannot learn every piece of music by heart, so could there be an easier method than the traditional way of transcribing music with notes? This was the starting point of the figurenote method, which set out to make learning music easier.

The figurenote method was created in 1996 by music therapist Kaarlo Uusitalo and together with music teacher Markku Kaikonen they developed applications and a method for learning music that used the figurenote method to help mentally disabled people. Uusitalo and Kaikkonen founded the music centre Resonaari in space that was owned by Helsinki City Council, and they began to teach music to special groups who for one reason or another were unable to participate in traditional ways of learning. Since 1998 they have received funding from the Finnish Slot Machine Association to developing research into the figure-note method and teach it to teachers and experts.

In the figurenote method the notes are separated from each other with different kinds of colours and shapes. The use of colour in particular makes it possible for mentally handicapped people and children to perceive the notes more clearly. Thanks to this, most people learn faster than they would in the traditional way. Additionally, this is an enjoyable way to learn that produces a feeling of achievement and raises the player's self-esteem and self-confidence.

All of this serves to increase the player's motivation. As a result of studying, the student's cognitive skills develop, information processing skills improve, and it becomes easier to picture the whole entity in its entirety.

The figure-note method also assists the development of handicapped people's social skills. Performing and playing together means paying attention to the surrounding environment and other players, and this makes it easier to act as part of a group. These kinds of experiences help handicapped people integrate as members of society and are not limited to a purely musical environment, they also improve social skills and make it easier to deal with almost all daily tasks. The figurenote method was originally created to help mentally handicapped people learn music, but based on recent experiences it has been noticed that the method is also useful for kindergartens and younger primary school children. The children do not just learn to play, they also get an opportunity to experience the joy of composition. In Japan there are ongoing experiments in using the figurenote method with elderly people who take part in organised daytime activities.

The figurenote method has also been researched academically and in many vocational education institutions, and it has even been the subject of a doctoral thesis.

Figurenote activity and cooperation has also begun abroad. At the present moment it is taught in Estonia, Italy, Japan, Ireland, Latvia and Scotland, and figurenote manual has been published in Japanese, Estonian and Italian.

The figurenote method is a social innovation which has made it possible for handicapped people and others to learn and enjoy making music.

Machiko Yamada – Ph.D.

60 STORYCRAFTING METHOD

The Storycrafting method is an important Finnish social innovation. Instead of necessitating many instruments, the demands for the use of the method are different: one needs to be equipped with a democratic approach to human beings, to both children and adults. Storycrafting is based on a premise that regardless of age, gender, cultural background, level of education, or degree of disability, we all have something to say. Together with an engaged listener anyone, from the young children to the elderly, is able to put their thoughts in to words in a story form.

While working as a psychologist in a school in the 1980's, I developed the Storycrafting method together with children. I withdraw from channelling children's interests to something specific with tasks or questions, and concentrated on listening to what kinds of issues the children brought up in their discussions.

The Storycrafting method differs from other narrative methods on the grounds on the four steps it includes. These are: a) evaluation-free listening, b) verbatim writing, c) reading of the written story, and d) making the corrections the narrator wants.

The recorder of the story needs a pen and a paper, and begins by describing how she or he is about to engage in listening: "Tell a story that you want. I will write it down just as you will tell it. When the story is ready I will read it aloud. And then if you want you can correct or make any changes."

In the Storycrafting method, the recorder neither channels the narration, nor judges the story. How the narrator expresses himor herself, should be up to his or her decision. The narrator should be able to decide what she or he includes or leaves out from the story.

Storycrafting is a method for recording stories in diverse settings: in pairs or within a group from intimate situations to public places. Storycrafting brings people closer to each other; it encourages and consoles. The experiences with Storycrafting method show that people often establish new profound levels and bonding in their relationships. Storycrafting halts the rush and assists in concentrating on the essential, namely, the words and the silent messages underlying the words. The power of the method relates to the fact that for a moment the narrator and the recorder engage in an encounter "on the same wavelength" as the ancient oral history narrators. In this mutual encounter, they fall into the stream of narration freely floating in the borders of dreams and realities. Storycrafting is an event of interaction where the recorder attains an access to the internal dialogues with the storyteller. The method is based on the notion that in addition to a general knowledge, each person has a wide array of subjective knowledge based on ones personal experiences. Because the quality of narration is free of judgments, Storycrafting gives an opportunity for the narrator to truly reflect on her experiences and thoughts with her own words.

The research on the use of Storycrafting method has shown that the culture of communication evolves towards genuine democratic relations between people. This change has wideranging effects. The voices of the silent individuals are heard and the talkative individuals become more interested in listening. The Storycrafting partners get to know each other in a new way: every narrative differs from the others and every narrator makes their own choice of words and arranges them in their own unique way. Even the smallest children use their own characteristic words and have their own ways of explaining things. Some have pearned to read and write through writing while others have gained the confidence that someone else is listening and understanding. It can happen between two people or in a larger group.Story crafting can be practiced telling story after an other story or by developing a common story, and it can involve drawing or composing music as long as the four criteria are fulfilled.

The Storycrafting has a bonding effect in relationships not only within close circle of acquaintances but also internationally. The awareness of other cultures and ways of living increases with the exchange of stories among narrators from different countries. A good example of this is the ongoing exchange among children in Finland, Palestinian children in Lebanon, children in Kirkuk, and Sri Lanka. Children participate the projects of Kissah Wa Tawasul (Lebanon), Prdi Chirok (Kirkuk), and Lotus Hill – the rehabilitation project of disabled children in Baddegamassa (Sri Lanka).

The Storycrafting method has been widely used for over thirty years for example in the Nordic countries and in Estonia. To name but a few of the fields of applications, the method has been used at homes, maternity clinics (innovation no. 39), day care centres (innovation no. 21), schools (innovation no. 52), libraries (innovation no. 51), hospitals, old people's homes, art projects and exhibitions.

It has been used among children, in office meetings, training, therapy, multicultural education, and solidarity work.

Monika Riihelä – Ph.D., psychologist

REGIONAL

61 NORDIC CO-OPERATION

The history of Nordic co-operation dates back to the 19th century and the Pan-Scandinavian movement. When it began in the 1860s it was mostly cultural and intellectual but by the end of the century judicial and legislative co-operation had begun.

At the beginning of the 20th century most organizations and movements forged Nordic relations and cooperation and after the First World War the Norden movement was created in association with all five Nordic countries.

In the period between the World Wars co-operation was established and a neutral Nordic foreign policy was proclaimed. The modern form of Nordic co-operation was initiated after the Second World War despite the fact that the Nordic countries opted for different solutions with regards to security and defence politics.

In 1952 the Nordic Council was established (although Finland was unable to join until 1955 due to the Soviet Union). During the 50s and 60s a passport union, common labour markets and a social treaty were created as a base for further integration.

A typical feature of Nordic co-operation, which has spread to almost every area of society, is that big projects that require governmental agreement, such as the common defence union (in the 1940s) and economic union (in the 1960s) fail, while grass roots co-operation that include the authorities as well as civil society organizations and which involve political parties and practical solutions that will benefit common citizens, become success stories.

During the 1960s and '70s the Nordic countries discussed a suggestion by the Finnish president Urho Kekkonen that the area would become a nuclear-free zone. Although this zone was never established it resulted in closer contact in the military field and a better understanding of each country's position.

At the beginning of the '70s, following the failure of Nordek, the official structures of Nordic co-operation were developed. Besides the parliamentarian Nordic Council a government-level Ministerial Council was established with a common secretariat. Ministers, as well as their government officials, began to meet regularly. At the same time the Nordic Investment bank was established. Already in the 1960s regional cooperation links were formalized and the Nordkalott co-operation began in northern parts of Norway, Sweden and Finland.

During the time after the Cold War the Nordic countries put a lot of effort into assisting the newborn Baltic countries and establishing many links across the Baltic Sea. At the same time the politics concentrated on European integration and the new membership of Finland and Sweden in the EU.

During the last decade Nordic co-operation has deepened again and is now dealing with questions related to globalization and security matters, but also classic inter-Nordic work which aims to abolish practical obstacles for citizens and firms.

Larserik Maggman – Sectetary general of Pohjola Norden 1998–2011

62 THE NORTHERN DIMENSION

The European Union has the Southern, the Northern, and a new Eastern Dimension. The central point here is that these are dimensions for all members and they require common policies by the EU. This was the idea when the initiative for the policy of the Northern Dimension (ND) of the EU was launched in 1997. It was stated in the conclusions of the European Council in December 1997 that Finland had initiated the policy of the Northern Dimension.

The first Action Plan was adopted in 1999. The ND became part of the EU's Russia policy and concrete EU-Russia collaboration in the area of the Northern Dimension on the basis of existing structures. It has created so far two important partnerships, the Northern Dimension Environmental Partnership (NDEP) and the Partnership for Health and Social Wellbeing.

The NDEP operates in three areas: environmental protection such as wastewater treatment, dealing with the Russian nuclear waste problem and environmental projects in Kaliningrad. The NDEP has resulted in the biggest single project so far with Russia, the construction of the St. Petersburg wastewater treatment plant, a 200 million euro project. It is the biggest achievement in the history of Baltic Sea environmental policies and the most substantial concrete cooperation underway between the EU and Russia. It will clean up the open waters of the Gulf of Finland.

During the project, the plant operator Vodokanal developed into a modern, efficient company. The plant's costs are going to be covered by levying charges on users, which is a novelty in Russia. The treatment plant sets the standard for the whole of Russia. This project opens up opportunities to participate in other similar projects in Russia.

Apart from investments and cooperation, it is also a question of priorities. With this project environmental improvements have moved to centre stage. President Putin has taken personal control of support for the Northern Dimension. It was also an important milestone in bilateral cooperation between the EU and Russia. The political and economic significance was underlined by the presence of the Presidents of Finland and Russia and the Prime Minister of Sweden at the opening of the plant.

Within the NDEP, a unique, effective international financing model has been developed by the Nordic Investment Bank (NIB). For the St. Petersburg waste water treatment plant project, 96.8 million euros were raised, consisting of financial aid by the EU, loans by international financial institutions – the NIB, the European Investment Bank (EIB) and the European Bank for Reconstruction and Development (EBRD) and also by many EU countries and Canada. The fund set up for the Partnership contributed 5.8 million euros to the project, but the significance of this was in the way that it committed the parties. Thus the leverage effect of the fund was almost 40 times as great.

The majority of the funding consists of loans taken out by the Russian side.

The other major ND-achievements are in the sphere of nuclear safety and support for Kaliningrad. The first five nuclear waste projects in the Kola Peninsular have already been launched. Implementation of the next group of projects is being set in motion at the moment. All this begs the question as to whether anything similar has ever happened in relations between the EU and Russia.

The second Northern Dimension Partnership created so far is for Health and Social Wellbeing, very much at the initiative of the Prime Minister of Norway Kjell-Magne Bondevik. The Partnership was included in the second ND Action Plan from 2004. It was a joint undertaking by the states in the region. Neither national borders nor those of the Union can prevent the spread of diseases. Currently 13 countries are members of the Partnership from Baltic Sea region, France and Canada. Apart from the European Commission, eight international organizations are members – as well as regional actors the International Organization for Migration, the International Labour Organization, the World Health Organization and UNAIDS, the HIV/AIDS programme of the UN.

The ND-Summit in Helsinki November 2006 adopted a new ND-framework document. The ND became a joint policy of the EU, Russia, Norway and Iceland. The ND is linked into the so-called four joint areas between the EU and Russia. The new document provides a political basis for practical work in the years ahead. The fact that Russia is more committed than previously means that more joint projects are on the way.

The new framework document opens up possibilities for new partnerships. They require a clear political commitment and the involvement of a sufficient number of partners. Finland has pursued the objective of establishing a transport and logistics partnership, especially since infrastructure, transport and logistics have been identified as the focal points of the EU-Russia Common Economic Space. Another theme is transport cooperation in energy efficiency.

I hope that international financial institutions, the EU Commission, Russia and other interested states – especially Germany, Poland, Sweden and the Baltic countries – will continue to press ahead with specific content and objectives for partnership initiatives. Hopefully USA and Canada will continue to make active use of their observer status and participate in present and future projects and partnerships.

We need to work with Russia in a spirit of partnership and equality in setting future priorities in our cooperation.

Paavo Lipponen – Prime minister 1995–2003,
speaker of parliament 2003–2007

63 TORNIO HAPARANDA TWIN CITY

"A border is not a barrier but a possibility." Councillor of Education Yrjö Alamäki's words have guided the twin city project between the Finnish city of Tornio (Torneå in Swedish) and the neighbouring Swedish city of Haparanda (Haaparanta in Finnish). A common history and cross-border family ties have naturally helped to dissolve the mental division, and, indeed, major barriers are generally only in our minds, not in the real world. And if there are true barriers, they must be removed. Working on this operational principle, Tornio and Haaparanta will once again become a single urban centre as if there is no official border between them.

The city of Tornio, which is situated at the head of the Gulf of Bothnia, was a city in the Swedish-Finnish empire from 1621 until 1809, when the Hamina Peace Treaty between Sweden and Russia "divided the Tornio Valley in a most unnatural manner between two states", as the governor of Northern Ostrobothnia, Ragnar Lassinantti, a true veteran of this regional cooperation, has stated. It took several decades before the city of Haparanda was founded in 1842 in territory that had earlier been part of the city of Tornio, which remained on the Swedish side of ther border.

Tornio-Haparanda's regional importance to Finland has been emphasised in times of crisis. During the First World War an air bridge was build between the towns to secure a supply passage between Finland and Sweden, and the region also provided important secret routes to Germany during the Jaeger movement. The road to Sweden also became familiar to thousands of Finnish refugees who had to take saunas (innovation no. 86) in Haparanda to get rid of their lice during the Second World War.

The post-war decades saw a shopping boom in Haparanda, as Finns raced over to Sweden for cheaper coffee and other groceries, and then, after the Finnish Mark was greatly devalued in 1967, the direction of flow was reversed as Swedes charged to Tornio for cheaper meat.

Fixed municipal cooperation started in the late 1960s with the joint use of the new Haparanda public swimming pool, and in the beginning of the 1970s a common wastewater treatment station and dumping ground were constructed in Haparanda nd Tornio repectively. This was a real boon for the municipality of Tornio, since the Swedish state paid 70% of the investment, and the two cities had to contribute only 15% each.

In the late 1970s the municipalities also made an agreement that permitted children to attend school in either country. This was contrary to the existing legislation, but it had been agreed with the Ministry of Education that they would turn a blind eye. In the mid-1980s the extensive cooperation was greatly intensified as a result of the foundation of Provincia Bothniensis.

Councillor of Education Yrjö Alamäki (Tornio) and his Swedish counterpart Bengt Westman (Haparanda) invented the idea of their "own province", which was governed by the president of the executive committee. Honorary consuls were also appointed in both Stockholm and Helsinki. In addition to the executive committee, the province has permanent cooperation bodies in all central administrative fields.

Cooperation was then intensified in various sectors. Currently e.g. all sport facilities are in joint use, the central heating system has been combined, and all major cultural events are organised together. The towns have a joint comprehensive school (innovation no. 52) which specialises in languages, an upper secondary school in Tornio which specialises in European affairs, and a joint tourist information centre, among other things. Tornio also plays all its Finnish ice hockey league games on Haparanda's artificial ice, and has won several Finnish championships there. The cooperation was expanded and continued until the mid-1990s when both Finland and Sweden joined the European Union, which allowed the towns to become physically closer when a security zone was no longer needed on the border. That gave rise to a new idea: the construction of a joint city centre on the border.

An urban planning competition was launched and the municipalities started joint town planning, but there were several setbacks in Haparanda as the residents considered the plan too expensive and doubted its benefits to the municipality. A referendum was organised during the municipal elections, and the border plan was narrowly rejected. Nevertheless, after the initial shock, the new Haparanda town council decided that the plan would be carried out with money acquired from the sale of land. A little later, Haparanda won a competition to be the location for a new Ikea, and when the giant store was located in the border area the gates opened and the project got off the ground on both sides of the border.

Roads, parks, dwellings, commercial business areas and hotels have been built and planned on both sides of the border, and the region is turning into a new, imposing central business district. The Tornio side has become the site of "Rajalla-PåGränsen", the largest shopping centre in northern Finland which has dozens of shops under one roof. On the Swedish side a market area has been built which was opened by Princess Victoria in 2011 and is named after her.

Apart from the Ikea and Ikano that are already on the Swedish side of the border, a huge number of business areas have also been buit nearby. As I write (in 2012) the towns have begun the construction of a joint travel centre (for trains, cars and taxis) on the border. Municipal areas are also being planned for the same area to be used by the councils.

The area has become a shopping Mecca for the whole northern region. A big building boom is under way and it looks like the original planned building time of 20–30 years will be halved. Belief in the future is stronger than ever and people are returning to their home towns. The change in the atmosphere has been astonishing.

Change is also based on attitudes, which must be changed first. The development of the towns' tourist maps is a good guide to the changes in the region. Even at the beginning of the 1980s the Tornio tourist map was colourful and nicely designed, but only on the Finnish side of the border. The Haparanda part of the town was only traced in grey lines to indicate that there might also be life on the Swedish side. The Haparanda tourist map on the other hand ended abruptly at the border. Now the towns have joint tourist maps, which tells its own story of vibrant life on both sides of the border.

Tornio and Haparanda are on their way to physical unification, which shows that ideas and visions can be realised if we only have faith in them and choose the right moment to realise them.

Hannes Manninen – Minister of regional and municipal affairs 2003–2007, mayor of Tornio 1973–1995

64. SPONSOR COMMUNE MOVEMENT

The sponsor commune movement between Finland and Sweden, which started during World War II, was a form of humanitarian aid based on voluntary civil activity. Sweden was eager to support Finland, and citizens wanted to participate. This desire was channelled through the sponsor commune movement.

It was not possible during the war to send every Finnish child abroad to be taken care of, but approximately 70,000 children moved to temporary homes in Sweden and Denmark. War orphans received help from individual people or communities that committed themselves to sponsoring a certain orphan for two years. Until 1958, Finnish war orphans received a total of 2.2 billion Finnish marks from these sponsors in Finland or abroad, for example from Sweden and the United States. Many Swedish people helped Finland in every way that they could. The collections organised by the sponsor commune movement enabled each citizen to give a little bit of money to this good cause without obligating them to other commitments.

Sponsor commune relationships were established according to a standard practice: one coastline commune was sponsored by another coastline commune, one industrial city by another, one rural commune by another.

There were a total of 653 sponsor relationships between towns, communes, cities and neighbourhoods. In Sweden the movement was organised through associations, while its Finnish counterpart was the local branch of the Mannerheimin Lastensuojeluliitto (Mannerheim League for Child Welfare). Relationships were thus based on civil activity rather than official channels. This arrangement also guaranteed that aid would not be used for military purposes.

Sponsor commune relationships were maintained by correspondence and visits that grew over the years into genuine friendships. Decisions on how to use the aid were taken together. Swedes were always kept informed about when the aid was received and how it was used. The goal of the aid was make long-term improvements in living conditions by e.g. hiring a nurse or building a health centre for well-baby clinics and the community doctor. The movement's slogan was "Help for Self-help".

The importance of sponsor commune aid increased greatly when, once the war was over, the financial aid allowed the importation of luxury goods, which were sold for high prices outside the rationing system. At first it was used to buy sugar. The so-called sugar crowns (named after the Swedish monetary unit) helped finance the construction of 500 commune health centres and the construction of 27 health centres for the Mannerheim League for Child Welfare. Sugar crowns also provided the initial capital for children's hospitals in Helsinki and Kuopio, as well as for many childcare centres. All in all, Finnish communes received about 1.4 billion Finnish marks as sponsor commune aid.

In 1946 the Norden associations in Norway, Sweden and Denmark started a friendship commune programme which was based on cultural exchanges between similar communes. The Finnish Pohjola-Norden association joined the programme the following year, and Finnish communes established twin commune relationships with their Swedish sponsor communes and partners in other Nordic countries.

Financial aid from Sweden to Finland came to an end in the 1950s and changed into cultural cooperation. Responsibility for this no longer lay in the hands of the Mannerheim League for Child Welfare. During the following decades the Norden associations cooperated actively, organising e.g. common visits, orchestra exchanges and sports competitions. As its activities were so similar, the sponsor commune movement was dismantled at the beginning of the 1980s and its operations were integrated into the Pohjola-Norden twin commune programme.

The sponsor commune and twin commune activities laid the foundation for Finnish communes' international activities and alleviated Finland's international isolation during the post-war period. Similar official twin commune relationships were also in later years established with other countries.

Aura Korppi-Tommola – Executive director,
Federation of Finnish learned societies

65 DEMILITARISED ÅLAND

30 March 2006 was the 150th anniversary of the signing in Paris of the first major international treaty relating to Åland. The treaty was signed by France and Great Britain and defeated Russia, and formed part of the peace treaty that concluded the Crimean War (1853–1856). In signing the treaty, Tsarist Russia agreed that it would never again fortify the Åland Islands. Unusually, the content of this treaty still applies, albeit in a new and expanded form as part of the new international legal order: the convention signed at the 1921 conference of the League of Nations in Geneva and the 1940 and 1947 peace treaties between Finland and the Soviet Union. Russia inherited the terms of the latter treaty in 1992. This makes the demilitarisation treaty signed on 30 March 1856 one of the world's oldest functioning military-political treaties in international law.

To understand why, we need to go back as far as 1809, to the peace negotiations in Fredrikshamn. Sweden lost the eastern half of the country to Russia, so Åland became the westernmost outpost of the empire. In 1830 Russia began the construction of the fortress of Bomarsund on the islands; this was intended to house a force of up to 8,000 troops at a time when the population of Åland numbered about 12,000. When the Crimean War broke out in 1853, the main fortress had almost been completed and could accommodate about 2,000 men. In 1854 the Allies dispatched a superior naval fleet in the Baltic to attack Russia. The target was St. Petersburg, but the Kronstadt naval fortress withstood the test, so the Allies turned their sights on Åland Islands. The capture of Bomarsund proved a brief and relatively simple expedition for the vastly superior allied forces, and once it was secured they destroyed it with gunpowder.

Sweden sought to recover the Åland Islands in the peace negotiations in Paris two years later but Great Britain and France preferred to force Russia to permanently demilitarise Åland. Thus the demilitarisation treaty, known as the Åland Servitude, was signed on 30 March 1856 in Paris.

Let us now jump ahead 60 years in our story, to the outbreak of First World War, when Russia demanded the right to partially remilitarise the Åland Islands due to the threat from Germany. Great Britain and France consented, and Sweden was informed. A number of defensive installations were constructed, and both Finnish and Russian troops were stationed in Åland. After the war, Finland declared itself an independent state as of 6 December 1917. Half a year earlier, Åland's political leaders had sought to reunify the Islands with Sweden; this evolved into what became known as the "Åland Islands Question", which turned into a difficult conflict between new-born Finland and her old motherland Sweden. Finland offered Åland autonomy, but the islanders declined. The issue was referred to the newly formed League of Nations in Geneva, where it was resolved in 1921. Finland was allowed to retain Åland, but it was obliged to safeguard the Islands' Swedish language (innovation no. 11) and culture through a more extensive

Autonomy Act (innovation no. 12). At the same time, a new treaty that also declared Åland a demilitarised zone was signed.

The demilitarisation of Åland was raised again in Geneva in 1921 and extended through a new convention with eleven contracting parties, including Finland but not the Soviet Union, which was at the time excluded from the League of Nations.

The special thing about the convention of 20 October 1921 was its 6th article, which stated that in times of war the Åland Islands should remain neutral territory, with no part of the Islands being used for any purposes associated with military operations that could pose a threat to another state. Åland would now remain demilitarised in peacetime and neutral in times of war. To safeguard the neutralisation of the territory, articles 6 and 7 authorised Finland, in the event of war or the threat of war in the region, to take such defensive military measures as may be required to ensure the neutrality of the Åland Islands. Finland has since come to regard this as a unilateral duty. Such military measures must immediately be reported to the League of Nations, a provision that has subsequently been taken to mean that the contracting States should be notified. Article 7 of the convention clearly defines the responsibility of the parties to maintain the neutrality of the Åland Islands for as long as war or the threat of war in the region continues. Under Article 7, the parties have a greater responsibility than Finland in this respect.

In 1939, on the eve of the Winter War, Finland and the contracting parties acted precisely as envisioned in the convention. Finland took the defensive measures necessary to secure the neutrality of the Åland Islands and also succeeded in keeping Åland outwith the theatre of war for almost the entire Winter War. The onerous peace treaty that Finland signed with the Soviet Union in 1940 included a demilitarisation treaty for the Åland Islands similar to that of 1921, with the exception of the neutralisation provisions Articles 6 and 7. In the Continuation War of 1941–44, the measures taken in 1939 were repeated, and Finland again kept Åland out of the war. Finland also managed to ensure that no invasion plans for the neutralised Åland zone, first by the Soviet Union and then, towards the end of the war, by Germany, ever got off the ground. Without Finland's defensive planning and the efforts of the Åland home guard, and without Articles 6 and 7 of the convention, the likelihood of these invasions actually being realised would have been much greater.

It is clear that, during wartime, the neutralisation provisions of the 1921 convention have had, and continue to have, a crucial importance in stabilising the Baltic Sea region especially with regards to Åland. The neutrality requirement is thus more important than demilitarisation, which applies in peacetime.

Åland's journey through the centuries has seen it evolve from being a pawn in the battle for its constitutional affiliation in 1809, 1856 and 1921, a demilitarised zone in 1856–1921, 1940 and thereafter, and an autonomous region of Finland from 1921, to become a neutral territory in the event of war from 1921 through Second World War until the present day – something that will hopefully never change.

Roger Jansson – Member of Parliament for Åland, 2003–2007

66 THE RESETTLEMENT OF KARELIANS

The Winter War and the Continuation War between Finland and Soviet Union ended with peace treaties (Moscow 1940 and 1944, Paris 1947) which obliged Finland to cede the Province of Viipuri to the Soviet Union and organise a massive evacuation of its Karelian inhabitants to Finnish territory, as defined in the Paris Peace Treaty. This cost Finland 10% of its territory. 44 municipalities, including 3 cities, were ceded to the Soviet Union, and the new border between the states divided 21 municipalities into two parts.

This was history repeating itself. For two millennia the Karelians have straddled two cultures, two churches and two great powers. Since the Pähkinäsaari Peace Treaty of 1323 the border between the two countries has divided both the Karelian people and their territory in two; the border has moved nine times, so there was nothing new about this.

When the Winter War ended in March 1940, a total of 440,000 people were evacuated from Karelia and thus obliged to leave their homes and possessions. When the first evacuees arrived in early autumn 1939, their resettlement was organised by local committees that had been founded for this purpose. However, the next January saw the number of evacuees multiply and arrangements were centralised to an *ad hoc* national organ, whose director was Urho Kekkonen, a Karelian mp who would later become President of Finland. In April 1940 the Karelian evacuees organised themselves and founded the Karelian Association to defend their interests. The Finnish Parliament (innovation no. 1) enacted the Prompt Settlement Act in June and a Compensation Act for property lost in ceded territory in August 1940. After the Continuation War in 1945 a complementary Land Acquisition Act was established. The resettlement legislation obliged Finnish municipalities, congregations and private farms to cede part of their land to the State, and these lands were in turn ceded to Karelians who had lost their own.

The execution of the legislation was entrusted to the Ministry of Agriculture's Resettlement Department, which was directed by Veikko Vennamo, who was himself a Karelian evacuee. The resettlement operation was huge in both Finnish and global terms, for no other country had carried ever out such a complete operation. The Land Acquisition Act included a Resettlement Programme for each municipality and town, which stressed the importance of maintaining former community and neighbourhood relationships. This aimed to relocate Karelians to regions which would resemble their former homes with regards to natural conditions, transport network and economic opportunities.

Resettlement was based on the free will of the people. People who had lived in e.g. the western part of Finnish Karelia were all resettled on the Finnish-speaking southern coast, but Karelians were relocated to every part of the country except the Swedish-speaking regions and the far north. On the insistence of Prime Minister

J.K. Paasikivi, a special language section was included in the Land Acquisition Act which stated that the relocation of Karelians should not change the language balance of the region.

Both the Act and the Resettlement Programme were agriculturally oriented and emphasised resettlement in Southern Finland and rural parts of the country. The size of farm allotted to each farmer was defined by the size of the farm he had possessed in Karelia. In general terms, farm-owners received the best compensation while landless people and urban workers were in a more vulnerable position. The situation was no easier for smallholders, who were relocated to small empty farms in infertile marshlands. Urban workers were better off, however, as growing towns were actually competing for a new labour force.

Things were difficult at first for both evacuees and their new neighbours, because Finland had only started to recover from the war. People felt homesick and found it difficult to adjust to their new conditions, neighbours and culture. Harassment, discrimination at school and cultural suspicions that lasted for years did not make things any easier.

Karelians looked to each other for support, which unified those who had earlier been divided into numerous subcultures. Orthodox fishermen from the tiniest village and fine ladies from Viipuri suddenly formed part of the same group of Karelian evacuees, and organisations and associations of people originating from the same parishes were founded to cherish Karelian culture.

The value of Karelian culture was generally recognised by the beginning of the 1970s. The ice had melted, and being Karelian was suddenly trendy. Finns have become more interested in their roots since the country joined the EU, and this upsurge in interest in genealogy has revealed that more than two million of Finland's five million inhabitants have Karelian roots. There is a growing interest in Karelian culture and traditions, which are even considered the cradle of Finnish culture. This is all because Karelians remained Karelians, never losing their identity despite the loss of their homeland. That is why every bakery in Finland, no matter its size, makes Karelian pies, a popular beer logo boasts the Karelian emblem of two clashing swords, and the Karelian anthem, composed by J. Hannikainen, is more popular than any other provincial anthem in Finland.

Hannu Kilpeläinen – Executive director of the KarelIan Association 2003–2007

67 FINNISH NON-VIOLENT RESISTANCE

At the end of the 19th century Russian nationalists began to call for a more systematic Russification of the country's borderlands, including Finland, which had been an autonomous Grand Duchy within the Empire since 1809. When N.I. Bobrikov arrived in Helsinki in October 1898 to assume the office of governor-general, he came with a firm conviction that the Finns had been allowed to cultivate the false doctrine of Finland's statehood for too long; constitutionalism and separatism must now be uprooted, and to this end he drew up a detailed agenda for the administrative and cultural assimilation of Finland into autocratic Russia. For many Finns the implementation of Bobrikov's programme was seen not only as a violation of Finland's constitution, but also as a coup d'état, "the instigation of military law," and the "murder of Finland." The Finnish resistance tradition was redefined and radicalised during the ensuing Finno-Russian conflict, incorporating a sophisticated variety of strikingly effective means of systematic non-cooperation. This "new way of waging warfare" was not understood simply as defence, but also as a kind of non-military warfare and nation-wide organisation with discerning offensive tactics. It was also conceived as a special Tolstoyan form of struggle.

Non-violent resistance was carried out through the constitutionalist front of the liberal Young Finn and Swedish parties, who were, in spite of ideological tension, joined by socialist labour groups. The constitutionalists' resistance organisation Kagal contributed financial aid to all worker-run, anti-government activity. Alongside students, workers were mainly responsible for stirring up agitation on a local level. A women's resistance organisation was also formed.

The basis of Finnish resistance was a refusal to cooperate with, obey, or recognise any unjust, illegal or violent acts committed against the Finnish people or their laws. Through this type of resistance the people were to wield a non-violent social power which would ultimately force the ruler into capitulating to their demands. To illustrate this, the resisters quoted Tolstoy's concept of voluntary servitude, which expressed the idea that if people do not make their sense of justice known in a firm and vigorous manner, and if they do not refuse to submit, then they have only themselves to blame for the oppression they suffer.

The Finnish resisters had a broad concept of the scope of the methodology of non-violent resistance. Popular education was seen as fundamental to societal defence, and another basic component of resistance was protest. At an early stage of their struggle, however, resisters emphasised that they had to go beyond protests, appeals, petitions and speeches to civil disobedience and non-cooperation, which they saw as the most important weapon in their non-violent repertoire. Furthermore, social and economic non-cooperation and social boycotts were advocated for use against both Russians and compliant Finns.

One early form of protest was to encourage prominent Europeans to protest en masse. Their success was impressive: twelve Pro Finlandia petitions to the tsar were signed by 1,050 of Europe's most outstanding representatives of literature, science, politics and art. The Pro Finlandia movement was seen internationally as a historically unique "activation of the public opinion of the civilised world."

On the domestic front an elaborate resistance organisation was established with departments throughout Finland. An underground press was created which succeeded in eluding official censorship with a wide variety of resistance literature – leaflets, booklets and newssheets – smuggled in from abroad.

Perhaps the most vigorous resistance campaign was against Russian efforts to abolish Finland's separate military and to conscript Finnish youths into the imperial armed forces. The conscription boycott succeeded to a remarkable degree between 1901 and 1904; no Finnish troops were incorporated into the Russian army and no Finns were obliged to fight in the Russo-Japanese war. The draft was suspended in 1905. A large part of the Finnish population participated in the unprecedented general strike that brought the empire to its knees in the Russian Revolution of 1905. Finns created one of the earliest and most sophisticated varieties of 20th century non-violent struggle, and M.K. Gandhi was watching.

Steve Huxley – Ph.D.

CIVIL SOCIETY

68 THE PROMISED LAND OF NON-GOVERNMENTAL ORGANISATIONS

There are approximately 90–100,000 registered non-governmental organisations in Finland, and these represent more than 80% of Finns. Most people are members of several organisations. The Finns, like their Nordic neighbours, lead the world with regards to participation, and the trend is rising: Finns founded almost 40,000 new NGOs between 1996 and 2010.

This associative tradition can be traced back to the latter part of the 19th century, or even to earlier times. Progressive groups such as the temperance movement and labour, youth and co-operative movements made participation in associations a self-evident way of fighting for a variety of causes and defining one's own identity. These movements combined intellectuals' endeavours to construct a nation and a state, and shape the Finnish population which was, from an international viewpoint, relatively egalitarian into separate social classes. As political democracy was thin on the ground, the associations assumed political functions, becoming the mouthpieces of different groups and regulating how they interrelated. After achieving universal suffrage in 1906 (innovation no. 7), Finns created a political party system and developed entire associational subcultures. Numerous associations, including women's groups, youth and children's clubs, senior associations, temperance and cultural movements, theatre associations, choirs, sports clubs and trade unions (innovation no. 71) affiliated themselves to local political organisations, especially the Agrarian or Centre Party, the Social Democratic movement, and later also the people's democracy movement.

Of course not all organisations were attached to the diverse array of ideological groups, but this certainly outlines the sphere of NGOs until the 1960s and 1970s. Between the World Wars, workers did not only vote for their own parties but also engaged in acting, singing and reading, and they bought their everyday supplies from and saved their money with their own organisations and companies. After the Second World War the people's democratic movement's organisations consolidated this structure. Even in the 1960s and '70s, many socio-political issues and international questions were crystallised in voluntary organisations. Hundreds of left-wing organisations, youth associations, critical culture organisations, friendship associations and development NGOs were founded every year.

This class and group-based organisational field started to collapse in the 1970s, and in the '80s Finns actively founded organisations which united individuals or enthusiasts in a certain field without paying any heed to great ideological divisions. This tendency strengthened in the 1990s. 60% of the organisations founded after the mid-1990s are cultural, sports or free-time associations, and people commit themselves to these organisations only partially, not with their whole personality as was the case with the ideologically-inclined associational subcultures. Associations for e.g. new types of sports, motor clubs or international pedigree dog or cat associations are part of "private" culture, as opposed to agrarian-oriented youth organisations or ideological women's associations, which link their members to a wider ideological context. They rarely arrange member recruitment campaigns or join a national umbrella organisation, but rather tend to base their activities on international patterns or their own model, which has been created by an inner circle. These organisational models are not learned from a larger group of associations or social networks, but are directly adopted from the media. In comparison to older organisations, new ones do not perceive their activities as permanent. They are also smaller, have weaker bonds, and are based on individual consumption or lifestyle rather than production and a common position in the labour market. The great majority of them strive to change their individual members' worlds, not the world around them.

This development is leading to a more apolitical sphere of NGO activities. As people commit only part of their personality to organisations, they cannot promote comprehensive political participation. Membership in a volleyball association does not exclude membership in a trekking association, as was the case with the scouts' and pioneers' organisations. It is however easier to become estranged from other people's problems when one has no experiential relation to them, as in earlier associational subcultures.

Nonetheless, the registered organisations still have political potential in this promised land of NGOs, which are not only the main channel of Finnish collaboration but also generate, harbour and transform critical culture and elements for new kinds of politics. The vast majority of so-called alternative activities have also been registered as associations, but unlike earlier times, many critical movements have remained unregistered. This might be a sign of a new era of participation. The phenomenon both underlines the current apolitical trend and also questions the tradition of registered associations in collective action. Instead of representative action, their essence is in subjective drive and loose forms of organisation.

In the 21st century also online networks offer a new kind of alternative to traditional organizations with virtual voluntary organization. In the future we will see if these will fuse into a single sub-group of innovative NGO activities.

Risto Alapuro & Martti Siisiäinen – Professors of sociology, Universities of Helsinki and Jyväskylä

69 ROAD MAINTENANCE ASSOCIATION

Private roads allow traffic from public roads that are maintained by the state and municipalities to reach private property. The owners of the property are obliged to hold a share in the private road that they use.

Share-holders have a duty to pay with their own money for the construction and maintenance of the private road, known as road maintenance. A private road is cared for by a road maintenance association, which is a special and possibly even unique arrangement which, just like private roads themselves, have remained unchanged in the way they are organized for decades. The same kind of model is in use in Sweden, however, and it is from there that the Finnish model has been copied.

Although shareholders in the road are bound to pay for the maintenance of the road themselves, roads that are deemed particularly important with regards to traffic and habitation receive grants from both the state and the municipalities. It is often a prerequisite for receiving a grant, however, that a road maintenance association has been established. A road maintenance association is advisable when there are many shareholders and the road requires regular maintenance. Road and road maintenance associations are governed by the Private Road Act. State assistance for private roads peaked at 35 million euros in the 1990s, but in 2012 this figure had dropped markedly to 13 million euros. The figure in Sweden is close to 100 million euros.

Finland has a huge amount of private roads – around 350,000 km – compare with the public road network which is only 79,000 km in total. Around 100,000 km is connected with permanent dwellings, 120,000 km is comprised of forest roads and 110,000 km provide motor vehicles with access to forests and summer cottages. Private roads that are considered important and fulfil the criteria for state funding comprise 55,000 km of the network.

The Private Road Act (1963) governs most matters related to private roads. This was preceded by another act which administered the roads in a way that was founded on public road laws from the beginning of the century. At that time public roads were at least partly the responsibility of local landowners, and they all had their own shares of the duty. As Finland is such a sparsely inhabited country, these roads have been both public rights of way and paths to serve local residents.

Finland has a somewhat special summer-cottage tradition which has supported the need to administer private roads while the rural population has been decreasing. There has been a need to travel on small roads in areas that would otherwise be regarded as being wilderness.

Finland has been for a long time and is still today Europe's most evenly inhabited country. Sweden, for instance, is otherwise very much like Finland, but it's population is clustered in villages, towns and cities, while in Finland the inhabitants are more evenly scattered.

The Finnish Road Association's new book *The Road Maintenance Association and shareholders* gives a good description of the system. The book's table of contents is a good starting point for understanding what the road association is all about, including road rights, road association administration, the principles of sharing duties, road association payments and funding organizations.

This has been a functional and democratic method which the old legal framework has supported for decades already, although it has not been able to stop a number of conflicts and differences of opinion that are rooted in common ownership. Having said that, however, the fact that the rules are regulated by law forms a good basis for the system to function.

Private roads can be maintained with only around a third of the costs of public roads. A growth in the amount of funding being awarded to private roads seems unavoidable because many private roads have become more important with regards to traffic while a number of changes in the population and ways of earning a living have made public roads quieter.

This means that the need to examine the borderline between public and private roads has increased, and it is hoped that new innovations will be created in the process. The issues that will need to be considered are the contracting and management of road maintenance and the role of local entrepreneurs.

The steps taken in recent years that have perhaps been most important were with regards to new road managers, who began to be trained in 2003–2004. There are now around 200 part-time road managers, 150 of whom have their own business.

Nowadays it is very much on the agenda to combine the maintenance of private and public roads to make the whole process more rational and effective. The idea is not, however, to find a single way of doing things, but rather to find the most sensible concept for each individual situation. Often this boils down to arranging the maintenance work in a rational manner and developing the terms of the management contract.

Lasse Weckström – Doctor of Science, former Director Genera of The National Board of Road and Water Works

70 FINLAND'S SLOT MACHINE ASSOCIATION

Slot machines arrived in Finland in the mid 1920s in the form of payazzo machines that were managed by German and Finnish businessmen, but it wasn't long before the public began to complain that private businesses were taking advantage of people's weaknesses. Pressure on the authorities grew so quickly that already in 1933 the state issued a decree giving charitable organisations the exclusive right to operate slot machines, but nothing much actually changed as businessmen still ran the show behind the scenes.

The Ministry of the Interior was not happy with this situation and in 1937 decreed that gambling machines could only be run by a new association which had been set up for this particular purpose – Finland's Slot Machine Association (RAY), which was established on 1 April 1938. At that time there were 670 slot machines in public use, and during the first nine months these generated 23.7 million Finnish marks (around 4 million euros), half of which was distributed as funding for 84 separate organisations. The new association had got off to a good start.

Contrary to other registered associations, RAY was from the beginning a joint project run by the state and NGO's to raise funds through gambling operations to support non-profit organisations in their charitable work.

The association created a network of representatives to make contracts with entrepreneurs – usually owners of licensed premises – and began manufacturing and maintaining slot machines, collecting the cash and managing the accounts. The association also dealt with funding applications, advised the government how the income should be distributed, and ensured that funds were used correctly, so it was involved from the moment the coin entered the machine until it reached its eventual destination. Funding was granted to all non-profit associations that fulfilled certain criteria.

As operations expanded, the juridical foundation of RAY's activities needed to be strengthened and, in the wake of lengthy preparations, a new decree on Finland's Slot Machine Association was passed in March 1962 which made RAY an "association under public law". RAY was bound more tightly to the state, but in practice its operations did not change much.

In spite of operational expansion and diversification, its initial principles are still intact – RAY continues to manufacture and maintain its own machines, it has a wide range of business partners, and it still submits a proposal for the allocation of funds to the government based on annual applications and supervises how grants are used. RAY's administrative board includes representatives of both the state and NGO's.

Operations have expanded rapidly with the opening of casinos in the late 1960s, RAY's own arcades in the late 1980s and an international standard casino at the beginning of the 1990s. In 2005 the turnover was 595 million euros and the profit – all of which goes to support non-profit activities that promote health and social welfare in Finland – was 404.5 million euros.

RAY can look to the future with confidence since this Finnish innovation has proven its competitivity according to all the indicators: Its activities are reliable, responsible and effective, and its profits benefit social objectives.

Markku Ruohonen – Managing director, RAY 1996–2006

71 UNIONISATION

The foundations of the Finnish trade union movement were laid in the second half of the 19th century when machinists, print workers and naval officers founded their first associations. However, only one in ten workers were union members in the first years of the trade union movement.

In the first income policy agreement (innovation no. 8), the so-called Liinamaa I that was signed in 1968, it was agreed that union fees would be collected directly from salaries and that they were tax-deductible. As a result of this the number of trade union members jumped dramatically and, after the first leap, continued to rise steadily. This peaked in 1993 when over 80% of all employees belonged to a union.

Labour market relations have a relatively strong position within the European Union. Tripartite cooperation and negotiations have also developed European working life. The position of labour market organisations is also recognised in the draft EU Constitution.

The enlargement of the European Union constitutes a major challenge to labour relations. The trade union movement is strongly committed to European integration, but the central precondition of successful integration is the development of the EU's internal cohesion. It is also a challenge for the credibility of employee organisations to reduce the social and economic differences between the new member states and old Europe. Integration must also mean safety.

The necessity of unionisation is accepted among all demographic groups, and young people's attitudes are also favourable in this respect. However, unionisation cannot be taken for granted in the future. The message of discussions held in the European Trade Union Confederation (ETUC) is clear: especially in new companies, the trade union movement has not been able to actively and effectively market membership. Numerous wage-earners have never met a shop steward in their working place. This means that the trade union movement is too focused on representing and defending employee's interests in traditional sectors such as industry.

In the future, the key is to go back to the workplace. The trade union movement has to earn its credentials again in a rapidly changing working environment. It has to find new lines of business and new workplaces.

Although the trade union movement's traditional role of defending workers' interests remains its leading sales product in European workplaces, the movement must be capable of responding to the contemporary challenges and even dreams of daily life.

A strong ability to defend interests, based on unionisation, is a common challenge for the European trade union movement. The larger and more unified group the trade unions represent, the louder their voice is heard in EU decisionmaking.

Despite high union density, Finnish trade unions have already woken up from a long sleep and started campaigning especially among young people who are only just entering working life. Active member recruitment campaigns and member services have become a fundamental part of trade union work.

Our message to young people entering working life is that unionisation matters. It matters what the wages and working hours are, how work and private life can be combined, and how retirement can be reached in good health. Who is it that takes care of all these issues? The answer is simple: the trade union.

Mikko Mäenpää – President of the Finnish confederation of salaried employees STTK

69 PARTY SUBSIDIES

Finland's State budget includes a fixed allocation for supporting party political activities. In 2006 this allocation amounted to 14,712,000 euros. It can be used, in accordance with section 9 of the Political Parties Act and section 1 of the Party Subsidies Decree, to provide grants to political parties which are represented in the Finnish Parliament (innovation no. 1), and to support their public activities as defined by their constitutions and programmes.

Party subsidies are granted by the Government (innovation no. 7) according to the number of seats held in Parliament. The decree provides that the parties allocate at least 8% of the subsidy to women's activities and 8% to district organisations, and earlier it was also decreed that another 8% should be used for international activities.

The Political Parties Act, which includes the party subsidy, was enacted in 1969. There have been some amendments to it, as good practice requires, but it is essentially in accordance with the proposal issued by Mauno Koivisto's government.

The central argument for the party subsidy is that it increases the transparency of political parties' funding. It aims to liberate parties from concealed private funding and the possible pressure related to it, and it has fulfilled this task fairly well. On the other hand, it is quite complicated to pressure a political party to make a certain decision. In general terms, any pressure is focused on individuals with a central role in decision-making.

The party subsidy system also aims to improve the stability and predictability of party funding, but having said that its real value has depreciated considerably since 1970. Only in the 2004 state budget was the allocation, which has fluctuated over the years according to State finances, tied to inflation. Since 2004, an extra subsidy of 10–20% has been granted in election years, and there is also a separate subsidy for information activities regarding European Parliament elections.

The party subsidy plays a significant role in party funding. For example, in the Finnish Social Democratic Party, it corresponds to around 45% of its income, including district organisations and the women's organisation. The base organisation and municipal branches however depend entirely on their own fundraising and member fees. It is often claimed that the party subsidy covers all the recipients' operative costs, but the example mentioned above clearly demonstrates that this is not the case.

In accordance with the above-mentioned Political Parties Act, the Ministry of Justice supervises how the party subsidy is used, as well as the legality of party activities.

The party subsidy has been both cherished and hated by the Finns – it has been used by several populist politicians to help them get wind in their sails. With regards to democracy, there are hardly any weaknesses in the party subsidy system. The composition of the Parliament is decided by the people, and the size of party subsidy granted to each party is defined according to the number of seats it holds. This makes Parliamentary Elections a real risky business for the parties and their finances, but one cannot, and should not, complain about the result.

The annual financial burden of the party subsidy currently corresponds to around two litres of petrol per citizen, i.e. around three euros. If this sum can significantly contribute to maintaining a transparent and democratic decisionmaking process in which each citizen over the age of 15 can participate even between elections, it is certainly not a financial burden on our nation.

A similar transparent and public subsidy system should also be created on the municipal level, because that is where most concrete political decisions are made in Finland (innovation no. 4). The municipalities also exercise significant economic decision-making powers in issues concerning e.g. town planning. A robust debate on the matter has started and I truly hope that concrete models will be realised in the near future.

A well-functioning party system is still the most fundamental element of democracy. An organisation can register as a political party quite easily in Finland, since it requires the support of only 5,000 people.

Risto Salonen – Administrative chief of the Finnich social democratic party

73 ECONOMIC AUTONOMY OF STUDENT UNIONS

After the Great Fire of Turku in 1828 the Royal Academy – the only university-level institution in Finland at that time – was moved to Helsinki. Along with the new statutes, the academy changed its name and became the Imperial Alexander University of Finland.

In its first academic year the university had approximately 340 students, but by the 1870s this number was already closer to a thousand. The basis of the Students' Association that originated in Turku maintained its form in Helsinki, albeit in a slightly modified fashion. In the early years the students convened at the university or in teachers' homes, but a wish for a "free atmosphere" led them to start holding their meetings in rented premises. Increasing rent costs then gave birth to the idea of a house that would be owned by the students themselves.

In its first meeting the student body, i.e. the Student Union, decided to build a student house. This would be financed partly by donated and collected money and partly by loans. The Student House (today known as the Old Student House) opened its doors on 26 November 1870. The students showed their ability to work as a team and their spirit of unity by first acquiring the piece of land needed for the building and then successfully completing the construction work. The Student Union, which was allowed complete freedom of assembly in 1880 and was now able to convene in its own building, developed into an organisation that united students representing different students' associations.

The income gathered from rent payments was first spent on the building and furnishing of the house, while later on it covered the maintenance of the building. When there was a need for larger-scale repairs or construction the Student Union took out loans against the property. The New Student House, which included business premises and offices that could be rented out, was built to meet the needs of the increasing number of students. The Student Union built its first business property in the 1950s, at which time it also successfully began its business activities.

The autonomous position of the Student Union, later known as the Student Union of Finland and since 1927 as the Student Union of the University of Helsinki (HYY), has always been defined by an act or decree. The leadership of the university has supervised the HYY's expediency but has not otherwise interfered in its activities. For a long period of time decisions concerning the HYY were made in public student meetings, but in 1932 this was transferred to an elected representative council. Officials, who were answerable to the HYY membership, were hired to take care of the union's essential administration.

In the Universities Act the purpose of a student union is defined as follows: "The purpose of the student union shall be to act as a liaison for its members and to promote their societal, social and intellectual aspirations and their aspirations regarding studies and students' status in society."

This definition is clear but fairly broad. The autonomous, activity-oriented HYY defines and renews its current and concrete tasks on a regular basis, either through the Representative Council or the Executive Board. The Representative Council set out the tasks of the HYY in its strategic plan on 27 April 2005 as follows:
- to unite all the students on the campuses and students' associations in such a way that each student feels that they belong to one united body of university students;
- to provide its members with services that make student life easier;
- to ensure that the organisations related to HYY have the means to function properly and to support the activities of the student body in a sustainable manner;
- to lobby on behalf of the students in the university administration, develop the university in cooperation with other groups within the university, and work for the benefit of the whole university;
- to influence decision-makers and public opinion in such a way that students' interests are promoted in the fields and forums that HYY considers important;
- to cooperate with other student organisations on a national level, representing students' interests;
- to help develop society in a proactive and responsible way, according to the values and thinking of the university students; and
- to produce academic professionals who are aware as well as critical thinkers.

HYY manages its finances based on long-term planning and a responsible attitude. This work is built on gradually acquired and well-maintained property, as well as business activities that have been developed in small stages. HYY's tireless work has provided its members – the students –

with a variety of services and benefits. As an autonomous association, it can independently decide what it wants to do with its assets and the profit from its business activities.

Linnea Meder – Financial director, former Student union of the University of Helsinki

74. THE COALITION OF FINNISH WOMEN'S ASSOCIATIONS

As its name indicates, NYTKIS – the Coalition of Finnish Women's Associations is the cooperation forum for Finish women's associations. The organisation is a significant social actor with regards to gender issues in Finnish society. It monitors women's rights, takes a stand on social and political issues, and strives to improve women's position in society and achieve genuine gender equality. Approximately 600,000 Finnish women are affiliated to NYTKIS's member organisations.

In 1987 a group of feminists, riding on a train to Moscow, started brainstorming about a women's organisation that would unite all women's groups from different sides of the political spectrum under one roof. The organisation would represent the Finnish women in international cooperation. A year later the women had already formed a committee. It was decided that the committee would assemble for a meeting as required, and all decisions would be reached according to the consensus. Presidency rotates annually from one organisation to another, and all member organisations are equally represented on the committee. In addition to the women's associations from the political parties, the National Council of Women in Finland, the League of Finnish Feminists unioni, and the

Association for Women's Studies in Finland are also on the committee.

Soon after the committee's foundation it became apparent that it was needed not only in international issues but also national politics. NYTKIS called for more women in the political decision-making process and organised the "Vote for a woman!" campaign before the elections. In the 1991 parliamentary elections Finland broke the world record on female representation in a national parliament, with 77 out of 200 seats being held by women. NYTKIS also organised seminars and training sessions, and reported to the authorities especially on issues related to women and family policies. This model of cooperation spread around Finland into regional committees.

NYTKIS's activities were for many years based on voluntary work, and they were mainly determined by the work contribution of each presiding organisation. In 2001 nytkis hired its first Secretary General, who put wheels in motion to register the committee as a non-governmental organisation. During the festive session, to mark the parliament's centenary in 2007, the Finnish Parliament (innovation no. 1) decided to establish government funding for women's associations.

Even at an international level, nytkis is an extraordinary coalition. It has been able to unite not only the political women's organisations, but also several politically independent organisations and promote their cooperation for common goals. The women's movement's agenda has not changed much over the last century; feminists are still striving to improve women's position in working life, stop violence against women, and promote the gender perspective in political decision-making and social activities in general. Today, a century after women won political rights, it is evident that even though they have come far together there is still a long way to go to achieve gender equality. That is why NYTKIS is working more actively than ever to promote women's rights.

Tanja Auvinen – Former Secretary General of NYTKIS

75 THE SERVICE CENTRE FOR DEVELOPMENT COOPERATION

The Service Centre for Development Cooperation, KEPA for short, was founded in spring 1985 as an umbrella for Finnish development non-governmental organisations (DNGOs). KEPA was born of two perceived needs: one was to breathe new life into the Finnish development corps following another very brief attempt at the end of the 60s. The other was the perception that the NGOs should take advantage of the broadly-based cooperation and positive experiences generated by the percentage movement and create more permanent and systematic structures for cooperation.

Development corps changed into a new form of development work in nearly all the industrialized countries. Educated youths with perhaps hardly any work experience were sent with hardly any money to participate in grass roots level tasks in developing countries. Gradually this changed to become increasingly demanding and professional salaried work.

As the development cooperation implemented by NGOs grew, it was decided that the time was right to restart the Finnish development corps' activities. There was one condition, however: its activities could be completely financed by public development co-operation funds, but the responsibility for the activities would be transferred to the Finnish NGOs themselves.

In 1982 an advisory board for NGO development cooperation (KaKeNe) was founded to coordinate not only the campaign but also lobbying on issues related to development cooperation. This body set up a work group led by Marja-Liisa Swantz, who was at that time the director of the Institute for Development Studies, to look at different ways of creating a permanent DNGO cooperation forum. In 1983 and 1984 the government appointed a committee to analyse the development corps' activities. The credit for the initial idea of KEPA goes to Marja-Liisa Swantz, who produced a memorandum for the KaKeNe working group which detailed the need for and proposed functions of a "Development Service Centre". The idea was that this centre's remit would include producing information and training services for NGOs, coordinating joint campaigns and serving as an "alternative consulting agency". The development corps committee decided to propose that the Service Centre for Development Cooperation take on an administrative role.

The rest is history, as they say. At KEPA's founding meeting was held on 5 March 1985 government and NGO representatives decided to "kill two birds with one stone", and found KEPA, which was charged with two principal tasks: to provide services and organise campaigns for Finnish DNGOs, and manage Finland's development corps.

This decision was typically Finnish in its aim to balance the needs and goals of the government and civil society in a way that would be "satisfactory to both parties". The Ministry for Foreign Affairs needed a representable organisation which would take responsibility for managing the development corps. The DNGOs had a different perspective, however: they thought taking responsibility for the development corps would allow them to start providing services and organising campaigns (thus receiving more public funding). In practice, the development corps became KEPA's main function while other activities were assigned to the back burner due to lack of funding. KEPA's actions were based on this concept for the first ten years that it existed. In the second half of the 1990s KEPA's activities were evaluated and the scope of its tasks was redefined – once again in cooperation with the Ministry for Foreign Affairs and DNGOs. The development corps became a separate activity and integrated into the new extensive programme focusing on the South, while programmes on information, services and development policy were developed into a versatile entity with much stronger resources than before.

KEPA is unique in the field of European development cooperation. The broad spectrum of the Finnish NGOs are ready to co-operate without prejudice or regard for the perceived divisions between organizations and at the same time engage in pragmatic co-operation with both government authorities and civil society.

In the mid-eighties KEPA began to nurture an offshoot which has stood the test of time: events called "Market of Opportunities". This is a bazaar-like marketplace event which has spread further across the country every year, and it makes development activitiesand NGOs better known to the general public. In Helsinki it is called World in a Village and has become a big annual multicultural event every spring which attracts tens of thousands of people to take part. KEPA still functions as the main co-ordinator of both the bazaars and the village events.

Folke Sundman – Executive director of KEPA 1986–2003, special adviser to Foreign minister 2003–2007

76 ONE PERCENT FOR GLOBAL SOLIDARITY

In autumn 1978 the members of a rural Southern-Finland Emmaus Community, which was well-known and widely respected for its fleamarket, austere lifestyle and work collecting clothes and money for refugees and orphanages in Africa and Latin America, went on a two-week hunger strike in protest against the low level of Finnish development aid.

Some friends of the community in Helsinki and other places started organising solidarity meetings, collecting signatures for a petition on the streets, and undertaking sympathy hunger strikes. The 1978 campaign was a success in terms of media visibility and activist mobilisation, but nothing much happened on a political level – the Finnish state budget for 1979 only reserved a miniscule 0.16% of the national GDP for development aid.

The Percentage Movement idea gradually took shape in campaign group meetings in Helsinki, and the initiative was launched in late autumn 1979. The concept was simple – everyone in Finland was invited to pay 1% or more of their gross income to support development cooperation projects or other solidarity work in the South which was undertaken or sponsored by a Finnish NGO.

With this long-term personal commitment, each individual participant in the movement added weight to the Percentage Movement's three basic demands:

1. Finnish state ODA (development cooperation funding) must reach 0.7% of the GDP by 1985. (Finland had, since 1966, repeatedly stated its commitment to this goal, which was set by the United Nations.)
2. Finnish development cooperation must be designed to benefit the poorest, most underprivileged and most oppressed peoples.
3. Paying 1% to development aid manifests a desire to move towards more sustainable lifestyle and development models in the North.

Between 1980 and 1984 the Percentage Movement was mainly furthered by so-called action groups, which were comprised of mostly young people and students who worked on an entirely voluntary basis.

The two most visible groups were in Helsinki and Tampere, but many smaller local groups were also active across the country. Gradually, as the campaign gathered momentum, both large and small development cooperation NGOs started to support the campaign and meet with the action groups. As the campaign became grew to become a real success story these meetings were attended by many experienced workers from across the spectrum of development associations in Finland such as the Red Cross, Emmaus, the Trade Union Solidarity Centre, the Missionary Society and many more. These meetings also seem to have contributed also to the forming of KEPA, the Service Centre for Development Cooperation (innovation no. 75).

The Percentage Movement also received voluntary support from many surprising sources, including a leading pr company that together with the action group mobilised a free media campaign featuring big adverts in leading weeklies and on television. All through the campaign the action groups encouraged people to pay their 1% contribution. They mobilised large organisations to support the campaign's principles and successfully lobbied well-known people from the Finnish political and cultural sphere to show leadership and publicly commit themselves to the campaign.

The groups also drummed up media interest, prepared their own publications, organised speaking tours and engaged in a great deal of political lobbying.

While the established development NGOs covered some of the activist groups' costs, the backbone of the campaign – its energy, ideas and political leadership – was the action groups and their weekly meetings which were held all the way through the 3–4 years of intense campaigning to plan and delegate work.

By 1983 more than 100,000 individuals in Finland, a country of around five million inhabitants, had joined the campaign, which was by this time very high profile. For example, when the final televised debate took place before the presidential election in 1982, all the candidates were asked whether they had joined the Percentage Movement, and all said yes.

During the 1980s Finnish state funding for development cooperation grew rapidly, reaching the 0.7% level during the late 1980s. It is of course impossible to say with any accuracy to what extent this was thanks to the Percentage Movement, but its success meant that the movement became less active towards the end of the 1980s. The Finnish ODA budget has since dropped to 0.35–0.45% over the last few years, but many Finns continue to contribute their 1% to the development or solidarity work of their choice. These contributions do not have the same political urgency or impact as they did 20 years ago, but we like to think that they remain important to how Finland as a nation and a people understands her responsibilities in the world.

Thomas Wallgren – Adjunct professor, Helsinki University

77 PEACE STATION

Why on earth are the premises of the Peace Union of Finland called the Peace Station? Because the beautiful two-story log building, which is surrounded by big concrete office buildings in the Pasila area of Helsinki, is actually a former railway station.

It was built in 1915 as Vammeljoki railway station in Karelia. After Finland became independent, the volume of traffic on the track, which ran from the former grand duchy to the former capital of the empire, St. Petersburg, via Vammeljoki, decreased. The underused building was thus dismantled log by log and rebuilt in 1923 as Pasila railway station, only 5 minutes by train from Helsinki central railway station.

In 1984 the Union's officials discovered that the Railway administration had organised an auction of Pasila railway station as it lay on the site where the new Northern Railway Station of Helsinki was to be built. A condition of the sale was that the old building had to be moved but conserved.

Next to the station, in the shadow of the concrete colossus, there was a kind of park that was originally planned to be a six-lane road. The Peace Union of Finland started to wonder if it would be possible to move the station building to the park, which would improve the whole neighbourhood and serve as a centre for its activities. The Peace Union of Finland put in a bid for the building and, though it was not great, it was enough to win.

On 8 September the same year the then president of the Peace Union, professor Göran von Bonsdorff, put the red cap of the station' s last director on his head and gave a startingsignal with the station's sign. This is how the "mobilisation for peace" began. The building was moved as a unit to its current position, only a few hundred metres away. The Peace Station weighed in at 150 tons and was the biggest building that had ever been moved as an intact unit from one place to another in Finland."It's just 10 tons less than a blue whale", shouted an excited small boy who had come to watch the operation.

The Peace Union of Finland was founded already in the Grand Duchy of Finland on 10 February 1907. In 1910 Senator Leo Mechelin represented the Peace Union of Finland at the International Peace Bureau meeting in Stockholm. The peace associations were banned by the Russian emperor during the First World War, but the union re-emerged in independent Finland in 1920 as the Peace Union of Finland – League of Nations Association. The activists chose this name to illustrate the union's ideology. It became relatively well-known, especially among intellectuals, but it had a difficult time in the 1920's and 1930's amidst extreme nationalist movements. After the Second World War the name was changed again to the Peace Union of Finland – UN Association, still illustrating the union's ideology which was based on international justice and supporting international institutions' work in promoting peace. However, members were getting older and the amount of activity was decreasing fast.

In 1963 academic circles founded a non-political peace organisation called Sadankomitea (the Committee of 100) in protest at political alignment with Cold War politics. This became a hegemonic student movement. Everyone wanted to join and wear the famous peace sign on their chest. This organisation came to the Peace Union's rescue in the 1970s when, acting on a proposal by the Committee of 100, the Peace Union of Finland became the central organisation for independent peace associations and groups.

The operation to move the building generated plenty of publicity. During the renovation a fire broke out in the building, which led the librarian of the Railway administration to state ironically that the building had stood up to two wars but had almost been destroyed in the hands of the peace movement. However, peace movement volunteers were full of energy and wanted to fix the damage caused by the fire and complete the renovation process in spite of the difficulties. This created an enormous amount of extra publicity.

The Peace Station has a prominent location, and its beauty and different style draw attention in a neighbourhood dominated by concrete. Most people in Helsinki know where the Peace Station is. The building was erected as the Peace Station in the 1980s, which was the decade of the international independent peace movement's successful campaign for European Nuclear Disarmament. The house provided the campaign with visibility, publicity and premises – just as it has for numerous other campaigns that have been organised by the peace movement over the years. The Peace Station has become a friendly and cosy citadel for all the new generations of peace movement activists. As its name suggests, the building is indeed a station of peace.

NGOs are considered important in the context of Finnish Democracy and they are financially supported without any political conditions. The City of Helsinki supports the Peace Station through subsidized land rent and the Ministry of Education provides an annual grant to facilitate its activities.

Kalevi Suomela – Honorary Chairman of the Peace Union of Finland

78. PROMETHEUS CAMPS AND THE YOUTH PHILOSOPHY EVENT

Many coming-of-age traditions give young people opportunities to develop their own sense of community away from their established roles at home and school and among their regular friends. In Finland, the Lutheran church's scripture school camp has retained its wide popularity in spite of the general secularisation of Finnish culture.

Finnish schools have offered comparative religion and philosophy classes since 1984 to pupils from non-religious families who do not want their children to take the traditional religious studies course. These pupils soon started to demand a true alternative to religious coming-of-age camps and in 1989 a group of them, together with their teachers, designed the first Prometheus camp.

A coming-of-age camp with a non-religious orientation designed by teachers would not really constitute a significant social innovation, but very soon the young camp participants from previous years were recruited to plan, orgsnise and run the camps. This created a unique atmosphere in which around twenty youngsters in each camp together with two volunteer adult guides spend a week thinking about and discussing challenging themes about life, society and the human condition.

Another innovative element is the absence of a guiding ideology or curriculum that should be learned during the camp. All the experiences, insights, thoughts and feelings of each participant, regardless of age, can be taken seriously and subjected to respectful criticism. The dialogue between the camp participants, the young assistant guides and the adult guides works because the programme has a good balance between thinking and discussing, experiencing and active doing. Nobody knows in advance where the discussions might lead.

Youths who participate in organizing Prometheus camps get an opportunity to shoulder real responsibility as they organize, plan and run an activity that usually requires highly trained adults. Without any big fuss they grow into their roles, cheerfully caring for their tasks, working with the group and each other as a team. They are able to face the strangest challenges and to confidently enter into serious discussion with unfamiliar authority figures.

The tradition of Prometheus camps gave birth to the Youth philosophy event, now an established tradition in its own right. The camp experience of a natural flow of dialogue inspired the idea of a big public event with speakers from the highest rank of thinkers, philosophers, politicians, scientists and artists who are invited to face the youths on their own terms.

I the youth philosophy event the speaker is first allowed only fifteen minutes on the stand followed by half an hour of dialogue with two well-prepared young opponents (aged 16–25), after which the whole audience can join in as well. The whole session lasts 90 minutes and often delves deeply into the speaker's theme. The main focus is a dialogue marked by mutual respect rather than trying to show off any superior knowledge.

The three-day event, organized in collaboration with students of philosophy at Helsinki University and teachers of philosophy and comparative religion and philosophy.

Both the Prometheus camps and the Youth philosophy event are strong, developing and growing even if they are not based on a commercial format or have the support of financial or political backers. The power of voluntary activity has given thousands of young Finns a unique opportunity to take a decicive step into adulthood without any ideological baggage.

Matti Mäkelä – Chair of the Prometheus Camp Association 2000–2005

79 COMMON RESPONSIBILITY CAMPAIGN

By the time the war ended in 1945, it had created a spirit of common responsibility in Finns and an understanding of the suffering of others. At the same time there was also an increasing feeling that that the Church should assume more social responsibility. In the post-war period, the main task of the Church's new welfare organisation was to distribute funds and goods received as aid from abroad. Another major challenge was the Common Responsibility Campaign.

In late summer 1949 the secretary general and secretary of social affairs of Suomen Kirkon Seurakuntatoiminnan Keskusliitto (currently the Church Resources Agency) visited the eastern and northern parts of Finland to evaluate the difficult circumstances created by crop failure and unemployment. The situation was dire, and the visitors were touched by the sight of malnourished and sick children. A decision was thus taken to start a massive national fundraising campaign that would be organised annually. Since the Common Responsibility Campaign was considered a continuation of public wartime fundraising which involved the whole nation, the President of the Republic of Finland J.K. Paasikivi was invited to be its patron. From the very beginning, the campaign has been always been opened by the President of the Republic of Finland with a speech on the radio or television.

The Common Responsibility Campaign has two important missions: raising funds for aid and giving a voice to those in distress. It also strives to open people's hearts and minds to distress in distant places that cannot be seen. Funds have been raised for international aid since 1963, and destinations and themes change on an annual basis. Aid has been distributed to widows, refugees, abandoned children, aids orphans, family caregivers, mothers with alcohol or drug problems and school drop-outs, as well as to developmentally and intellectually disabled, elderly, starving, unemployed, deeply indebted and homeless people and to those with mental health problems.

Every year the campaign produces, in cooperation with other social actors, material to support ethical education in day-care centres, schools and church congregations.

Apart from this ethical education and fundraising for international aid, the campaign's mission is to influence politicians and policies. In the 1990s the Church became more vocal in its social criticism; the most renowned example of this was the Church's famine group, which was created as part of the Common Responsibility Campaign's food bank project.

The campaign's vision can be summed up as follows: it is the common creed of the Church as a whole, an act of love for a world in distress; it is a socially significant advocate of justice and forgotten groups of people. The Common Responsibility Campaign is the most renowned and extensive citizens' fundraising campaign, and it constantly updates its image and modes of action.

The Common Responsibility Movement is close to the population's heart. Every year it offers tens of thousands of Finns a clear way to act to help their fellow men and women. The Movement does not seek out easy and so-called honourable aid targets but rather targets groups that are most in need of help and who would not otherwise receive help. Those who have been forgotten and marginalized become visible and receive help from the Common Responsibility Campaign and the collection. It is Finland's oldest and largest annual public collection, and it has survived because it is not afraid to change and move with the times.

Kalle Kuusimäki – Former fundraising director,
Church Resources Agency

80 OPERATION HUNGER DAY CAMPAIGN

"It feels good to follow the Operation Hunger Day nowadays. I'm really glad that the idea spread like this", 82-year-old Mailis Korhonen from Pälkäne rejoices. 27 years ago in the heart of Häme Province she organised an event which grew to become the biggest annual collection arranged by the Finnish Red Cross to augment the Disaster Relief Fund.

In November 1980 the Red Cross flags waved in the centre of Pälkäne. Korhonen, who was at that time president of the Pälkäne branch, and Erkki Korkama, the executive director of Häme, had contemplated new collection ideas and come up with a new method: healthy adults from Pälkäne could live for a day completely or partly without food, and give the saved money to help the starving.

"It was not at all difficult to get people to participate. Everyone was really positive about the idea", Korhonen remembers.

The Operation Hunger Day and the Disaster Relief Fund are unique Finnish inventions.

During Operation Hunger Day funds are raised for the Finnish Red Cross Disaster Relief Fund, which allows the organisation to respond quickly and efficiently to the need for aid in catastrophe areas around the world. The fund also finances long-term development cooperation and aid work in Finland, and it enables a more immediate response to disasters.

Operation Hunger Day is still the most important collection organised by the Finnish Red Cross for the Disaster Relief Fund. During the operation, normal Finnish people give aid to other normal people who need it in other parts of the world.

The event has been transformed from a traditional box collection in market places to become a massive collection and information campaign which is visible in every part of the country in e.g. streets, schools and working places. The collection has become one of the Finnish Red Cross's biggest voluntary operations; in 2005 there were almost 25,000 volunteers out collecting money in the streets.

Since 1981 Operation Hunger Day has made approximately 54 million euros, which the Finnish Red Cross has used to help people in numerous disasters. For example, in 1984 the aid was channelled to Africans suffering from ongoing famine, and after seeing images of their distress the Finnish people really threw their weight behind the operation's position. Aid has also been given to victims of civil wars and other conflicts, to refugees' resettlement and to people affected by natural disasters around the world.

In Finland the Finnish Red Cross Disaster Relief Fund has funded assistance for people after sudden accidents, e.g. people injured in major bus accidents or in the Asian tsunami in December 2004.

The Finnish Red Cross maintains the Disaster Relief Fund in order to respond as rapidly as possible to the need for aid. The fund is constantly open to collect donations which the donor has not designated for a certain purpose.

The Red Cross can thus provide aid immediately after it has been petitioned.

Aid can be supplied as money and provisions, but also as expert work. For this purpose, the Finnish Red Cross maintains a register of more than 500 people, including specialists from all the professional sectors including medicine, water supply and sewerage, financial management and communications.

More than 90% of donations to the Disaster Relief Fund come from private donors. The rest is given by businesses and other organisations. Out of all Finnish Red Cross collections, Operation Hunger Day adds most to the Disaster Relief Fund. Doing their own fundraising also guarantees, in addition to the rapid delivery of aid, that the aid is independent and impartial. The Red Cross delivers its aid to those places where it is most needed.

The organisation's own experts estimate how much and what kind of aid is needed, and it is then delivered through the organisation's own network.

Thanks to the Disaster Relief Fund, the Finnish Red Cross has a logistic centre in Tampere where there are always blankets and clothes ready for immediate shipping – as well as two fully equipped camp hospitals. The fund also covers the expenses incurred by relief aid workers who have been sent to catastrophe areas.

Hannu-Pekka Laiho – Communications director,
Finnish Red Cross

HI-TECH

81 LINUX

When 21-year-old Linus Torvalds started developing his own unix-based pc operating system, he hardly imagined that he would challenge the world's mightiest operating system corporation Microsoft and end up an idol of computer enthusiasts around the world.

The decisive moment for Linux was when Torvalds decided to upload the source code of Linux's first version to the Internet and let anyone download, use and develop it. All that Torvalds asked in return was feedback from Linux users.

He received oceans of it, and soon there was an Internet network of thousands of volunteers working with Linux in over 90 countries. However, without Linus Torvalds, the network would have lacked a direction and goal.

Linux's greatest innovation of is not therefore technical but social. What at first might appear as an anarchic and volunteer-based Linux community has been able to create an efficient and innovative organisation whose members are uniquely motivated and committed to develop and maintain Linux.

The Linux community is a fine example of new network organisations being enabled by communication technology. The vast majority of those who have participated in developing Linux have never met each other – except through the Internet.

Linux is the most famous open source programme in the world. Open source programmes have to comply with the criteria established by the Open Source Initiative, the main principle being that everyone must have free access to both the programme and its source code. Everyone is entitled to modify the programme as they wish, providing that the modified source code is also freely accessible, and that it can be further modified.

This is in stark contrast to commercial software development, where source codes have traditionally been jealously guarded business secrets, which means that they cannot be exploited elsewhere and that users cannot evaluate the quality of their programmes. In widely used open source programmes like Linux, every single row of the source code is analysed by a mass of people. Testing is much more profound than commercial programmes' quality control, and Linux is consequently known for its reliability and speed. The People's Army of China, for instance, decided to use Linux mainly because they can check for themselves what their computers' operating system is doing.

Linux and other open source programmes have become especially popular in developing countries, where people cannot afford to pay for licences for commercial programmes, and because Linux functions in old computers which are still used in developing countries. If a particular function is missing, local people can always programme it by themselves.

Although Linux itself is freeware, it has also generated business and commercial services. For example, ibm, Sun and Novel use it in their servers and have invested millions in developing Linux, and many "embedded systems" like mobile phones and video recorders also use it. In addition, 70% of the world's 500 fastest computers use Linux as their operating system.

Linux is however still used relatively rarely in personal computers, mainly because its installation has required considerable computing skills. Even though distribution packages have been developed to facilitate installation, it is still quite complicated.

Linux and other open source programmes have recently also become a political issue, as public authorities' data systems have been criticised for becoming too dependent on software company's products. The result is likely to be a stalemate: open source programmes will be more frequently used, but at the same time commercial software companies will improve the compatibility of their own products – even with open source programmes.

Jyrki J. J. Kasvi – Techn. D. Member of Parliament 2003–2011

82 SMS MESSAGING

Nowadays more than 3 billion GSM customers across the globe use SMS, Short Message Service, at work or just for fun. The most important features of the SMS are directness and speed, as well as the brevity of the message. Apart from being efficient, short messages are also polite they can be received without creating a disturbance and answered when appropriate.

The idea of text messaging was born step by step. One ancestor of SMS is telex, which was still commonly used in the 1980s before e-mail and electronic phones arrived on the scene. Another root is the paging systems that were popular at the beginning of the 1980s. The beepers were able to receive text but the only way to send it was to dictate the text to an operator, who would then pass it on. It was clumsy to use and expensive for both the customer and the operator so the service never took off.

The huge success of Nordic Mobile Telephone (NMT) inspired the Nordic telecommunications authorities to initiate a joint working group "FMK" in 1981 to develop future digital mobile communications.

Engineers enthusiastically set out to develop radio technology that would be useful in everyday life, their ultimate goal being a multi-purpose pocket phone, which at the time was regarded by many as something of a joke.

The first time that I realized that short text messages between mobile phones would be a useful device was in a brainstorming session with Juhani Tapiola and Seppo Tiainen in Copenhagen in the early 1980s when we met the evening before the Nordic project had sub-group meetings to prepare ourselves and discuss the feartures we hoped would become part of futute mobile communications (FMK).

Juhani Tapiola was mainly concerned with the difficulty of sending text messages to pagers, I was a firm believer in pocket phones, and Seppo Tiainen usually had a quick grasp of how an abstract idea could be concretely realised. First we concluded that the future system should enable messages to be dialed from pocket phones to pagers. Juhani Tapiola took a programmable HP calculator tfrom his pocket to prove that the number of buttons needed to write messages with a small tool would not be a problem. Soon I realised that the whole paging system was unnecessary as the same mobile phone could also receive incoming messages. We excitedly made a list of different uses for text messages and invented a Finnish name for our system: "tekstinäpellin".

Of course, back then we never dreamt that in the space of 15 years text messages would be an everyday tool, not only for business but also for families and children everywhere around the world.

At the same time as FMK was planning the first pieces of the modern mobile communication jigsaw, the same thing was also happening among many other national and international development teams. Text messages were also being considered in a Franco-German collaboration, and when European efforts were gradually moved into one organization (Group Special Mobiles (GSM)) the Franco-

German proposal for a text service (SMS) was worked into the final specification.

The existence of SMS is based on the rapid development of enabling technologies, the free sharing of information, a huge joint effort to specify the new services and systems and the unselfish work of thousands of individuals. The international telecommunications field in the 1970s and early '80s regarded the free sharing of ideas as a virtue and an absolute requirement.

As a social innovation, text messaging may be legitimately called Finnish. In the mid-1990s, when SMS was widely available for mobile phone users, Finland was the leading country in offering mobile services. In Christmas 1996 the operators' network collapsed under the weight of so many people sending their Christmas greetings by SMS, and the same thing happened later elsewhere.

Matti Makkonen – Pioneer in mobile services

83. IRC (INTERNET RELAT CHAT)

IRC was born in August 1988 in the Department of Information Processing Science in the University of Oulu. I was starting my third year as a student in the Department of Electrical Engineering and was a summer trainee in the Department of Information Processing Science. My instructor Heikki Putkonen made me the administrator of OuluBox, a BBS system which was free for anyone to use through a modem or via the university computer network. Discussions could be held with other OuluBox users by leaving messages for others to read, and, as it could be accessed through the university network, it was possible to have scores of simultaneous users.

I originally developed IRC as a solution for OuluBox's real-time discussion needs. IRC was influenced by an mut (Multi-User Talk) programme that had been developed by Jukka Pihl and was used for a short time as OuluBox's realtime chat programme before IRC superseded it. IRC was a distributed system from the start, so multiple IRC servers have always been able to form a common IRC network. Each user connects to a server, and the servers relay the messages from one user to another. The IRC network therefore consists of several equal servers. This real distributability and lack of central control is probably the most important technical reason for IRC's popularity;

it was the deciding factor when IRC was compared at the time with several other Internet chat programmes.

IRC spread within Finland first; Helsinki University of Technology, Tampere University of Technology, the University of Jyväskylä and the Technical University of Tampere were the first IRC server locations after Oulu.

Servers from the University of Denver and Oregon State University were the first non-Finnish servers to join the IRC network, which then spread quickly to every continent. Tens of people were now actively participating in IRC development following Open Source software development principles.

In the beginning many universities and departments, including the Department of Electrical Engineering in the University of Oulu, prohibited the use of IRC due to the fact that users tied up computer terminals for hours on end, keeping other students from their programming assignments.

In 1991 ordinary people from e.g. Israel were using IRC to send reports about the first Gulf War to every corner of the globe.

IRC has had an effect to the personal lives of tens of thousands of people the world over. Many have found their partners through IRC and numerous minorities (e.g. sexual, political, social) have formed societies to allow members to discuss things freely with other like-minded people.

Nowadays there are hundreds of local and worldwide IRC networks, and the number of users is counted in millions.

Jarkko Oikarinen – Ph.D.

84 THE MOLOTOV COCKTAIL

In autumn 1939, a couple of weeks before the Winter War began, the Ministry of Defence ordered a load of empty bottles from the Finnish state alcohol monopoly Alko (innovation no. 33), and these requests became more frequent after the war started. When Matti Inkinen, a graduate engineer who was at that time the director of Alko's central supply, inquired from Major-general Oiva Olenius, the head of the Ministry of Defence, where the bottles were going, the reply was that the army used them to make petrol bombs for the front line as they were basically the only means of anti-tank defence the Finns had at their disposal. They had proven themselves effective, although soldiers found filling the bottles slow and complicated.

The bottling lines in Alko's factories were standing practically idle at the time as Alko shops were closed because of the war and its employees were away fighting at the front, so Inkinen realised that Alko could help the army; Alko factories in Rajamäki soon started producing petrol bombs, a mixture of alcohol, gasoline, petrol and tar, which were nicknamed Molotov cocktails after the Russian Minister of Foreign Affairs. The army delivered the petrol, and the Bengal fire sticks needed to light the contents were supplied by five different match factories, mainly the Match Factory in Pori.

The petrol bombs, satchel charges and box mines manufactured by pioneers compensated for the shortage of anti-tank artillery, especially in early battles; Juho Niukkanen, the Minister of Defence at the time, states in his memoirs that more than half of the enemy tanks that were destroyed were hit by these crude instruments, the use of which required a great deal of bravery. The consequences of a Molotov cocktail strike were devastating – once the bottle broke, the burning sticks lit the fuel and the tank burst into flames and was destroyed, even if it hadn't been directly hit.

The fuel mixture was later developed to make the liquid stick better to the tank's surface, and the lighting mechanism was also improved.

During the Winter War a total of 542,192 petrol bombs were bottled in the Rajamäki factory by the 87 women and 5 men who worked there. As a result of their work, however, the factory became a target and was later bombed. And no wonder really – the first bottles had been closed with tops that gave the exact address: Alko – Rajamäki.

Heikki Koski – Managing director of Alko 1982–1994, Minister of the Interior 1975

EVERYDAY
AMUSEMENT

85 WORKING BEES

In Finnish society, voluntary work in the form of working bees is an important form of production and social interaction. The objective of working bees has generally been to complete a large important task that requires a considerable work contribution, so neighbours, acquaintances and relatives are invited to participate.

The essential thing about working bees is that they are purely voluntary in nature and no money changes hands. Neither is there any direct obligation to return the favour.

Traditionally, participants were rewarded with good food and drink, and there would generally be a sauna (innovation no. 86) when the working day was over, often followed by a dance, so it was an occasion to have some fun together. Working bees had a considerable impact on improving production and productivity but, above all, they strengthened the community spirit.

There is probably no sphere of life in which working bees were not organised, but the most common tasks were farming work, such as harvesting, hay-making and bringing in the potatoes. Working bees were also a common way of organising construction, for transporting timber or building walls or roofs, and launching and storing boats and hauling firewood are other typical examples. Construction bees mainly concerned men, spinning and carding wool was typical women's work, and everyone would work together to bring in the harvest, gather flax and thresh cereals.

Although work was not specifically asked in return, the working bee system can be viewed as being based on an unspoken agreement within the community, according to which each member could count on the help of neighbours to perform group tasks. Working bees have been an efficient way of organising work that would have required a massive effort from individuals or households to manage on their own, and some of this work would probably have ended up being left undone. Harvesting and hay-making, for instance, must be completed in a relatively short space of time, and working bees facilitated the quick execution of these urgent tasks; the Finnish climate demands that hay-making be completed within two weeks.

Young people's evening gatherings, where girls would do needlework and young local men would come for a visit, can also be considered a form of working bee.

In south-western parts of Finland there were also other forms of mutual assistance through which certain village households would regularly help each other to make hay in distant meadows and with harvesting and threshing, and similar established working unions also existed among relatives living in different villages. Another form of cooperation through working bees has been traditional catering circles, whereby villagers would help each other in family celebrations and other parties with both the food and other practical tasks

Reino Hjerppe – Emeritus director general,
Government institute for economic research

86 SAUNA

There are over two million saunas in Finland – enough to accommodate every Finn, even if they all wanted to go at the same time! Although the Finnish sauna was originally a rural phenomenon, the tradition spread to the city long ago, initially in the form of public saunas and then as private installations in urban dwellings. Nowadays saunas are even built into tiny one-room apartments.

Throughout the world, Finland is known more for its sauna than anything else. The word itself is known in over a hundred foreign languages, more than any other Finnish word. Even though Finns did not actually invent the sauna, their attitude towards it has always been unique. Sauna has been considered a sacred place, a source of many myths and folk beliefs, and a certain devotional attitude towards it has survived right up until the present day – a well-known proverb says that one should behave in the sauna as if one is in church.

Sauna is present in every area of Finnish culture, in both science and art; there have been close to 20 doctoral theses and hundreds of other publications on the physiological and medical effects of sauna while, apart from being a subject for music and visual art, it is mentioned dozens of times in the Finnish national epic Kalevala, and practically every important Finnish writer has described bathing in the sauna. A really popular television talk-show, in which the two male hosts invited famous people to take a sauna with them, ran for years, and dozens of government ministers and members of parliament, including the current Finnsh president Sauli Niinistö and his predecessor Tarja Halonen, participated in the programme, generally wrapped only in a towel.

Even though a typical rural sauna looks very different from mass-produced and corporate versions, the procedure itself has remained unchanged for centuries. It is based on alternating hot and cool: one first spends 10 or 15 minutes in the steam room, which is heated to 80 or 100°C by a stove. The steam or "löyly" is created by throwing water on the hot stones which fill the stove. Bathers may also beat themselves with a bunch of leafy birch twigs. One then cools down by sitting outside, taking a shower, swimming, or rolling in the snow. This cycle of hot and cool is normally repeated two or three times, but can go on for as long as desired, and the bather finishes off with a wash.

On average, Finns are introduced to the sauna when they are around 20 weeks old, and they will take a sauna every ten days or so for as long as they are physically capable. In bygone times the sauna was an essential part of many events in Finnish people's lives: giving birth, cooking, making clothes, taking care of the sick and preparing the deceased for their final journey. Nowadays, however, Finns take a sauna primarily to relax. Ex-president Urho Kekkonen – a great friend of the sauna – crystallized the feelings of many Finns when he said: "In the sauna I relax physically and invigorate mentally. The calm atmosphere creates harmony. For me, life without a sauna would be completely impossible."

Lasse Viinikka – Honorary President of the Finnish Sauna Society

87 SANTA CLAUS

On Christmas Eve, all over the world, millions of children wait for a visit from a friendly, whitebearded, red-coated old man, but the role of the Finnish Santa Claus as a gift-bearer is in fact relatively new. The Finnish word for Santa Claus – joulupukki, literally 'Christmas goat' – still brings to mind the creature that preceded the jovial old man the goat that symbolises both fertility and the devil. In bygone festive parades that called from house to house there were generally horned goats that did not bring presents but on the contrary had to be fed, and the creatures that ran around at New Year celebrations can be traced quite far back in European tradition.

In Finland, carnivalesque goats were still around even in the 20th century. In eastern and north-eastern parts of the country, the harvest celebration, kekri, included the visit of a goat that would sharpen its nose made out of shears to frighten the children and threaten to capsize the stove if it wasn't given anything to eat. On St. Thomas' Day, a figure called Risu-Tuomas (Twig Thomas) roamed the towns of western Finland with a gang of disguised youngsters in tow who would inquire if there were any bad children in the house and ask for something to drink. The Christmas goat also appeared on Christmas Eve, with a birch-bark mask, beard and horns so that it resembled a real goat.

Children accompanied the goat from house to house, dancing, cracking jokes and partaking of hospitality. The inhabitants of the house might also receive presents, but they were brought by someone else who would often just throw then in through the barely open door.

In Häme province youths amused themselves on St. Stephen's Day by going round the houses asking whether Stephen was at home. The St. Stephen's Day goat was dressed up in a fur worn inside out, wooden horns, and had a bath whisk for a tail. In Karelia a smuutta or ropakko wandered around between Christmas and Twelfth Night. It tried to avoid recognition by changing its voice and manner of speaking, but actually entering a house protected in this disguise provided a good chance to patch up old quarrels. After Twelfth Night, nuuttipukki goats rambled through the villages of Häme and south-western Finland, taking the tap from the barrel if they were denied the home-brewed beer they demanded.

According to legend, St. Nicholas served as a bishop in Myra in south-western Turkey in the 4th century, and was respected in both in the Eastern and Western Churches. He was adopted as the protector of especially sailors, fishermen, merchants and people living on islands. In the Nordic countries he was among the most important Catholic saints in the Middle Ages, in Finland after the 12th century. He then became a more popular figure in Finland, being made protector of the birds, Master of the North and a forest deity. However, on a global scale, St. Nicholas is more renowned as the precursor of Santa Claus, as the source of a long success story. In paintings St. Nicholas was occasionally portrayed in a red cloak, and on St. Nicholas' Day, the 6th of December, he might appear in scenes as a figure sharing sweets with children. Dutch Protestants took St. Nicholas with them to New Amsterdam (New York) and other parts of the United States, and during the 19th century he gradually turned into Santa Claus, the patron saint of Christmas markets and presents, a fairytale figure that sped through the sky with his team of reindeer, climbing down chimneys at night to put Christmas presents into children's stockings. Old England's Father Christmas, Protestant Germany's Weihnachtsman and Russia's Ded Moroz are all partly descended from St. Nicholas, and the Finnish Santa Claus is also a part of the same brotherhood.

In eastern Lapland there is a mountain called Korvatunturi – literally Ear Fell. The name suggests that the mountain can hear whether the children are being well-behaved or not, and although Markus Rautio, a popular narrator of children's radio programmes, maybe did not personally come up with the idea of Santa living in Korvatunturi, he certainly reinforced this idea in the late 1920s. Another important factor in the spread of Christmas traditions was the primary school system. By this time our Santa had already got married and lost his horns, even though he might still go from house to house in a lamb's fleece, and he had also recruited a gang of elves to help him. These little creatures were akin to the elves that in Finnish folklore protected houses and other buildings, and they were perfectly suited to observing children's behaviour since their earlier mission had been to promote good morals.

In his designs for a Coca-Cola Christmas campaign in the early 1930s, American Haddon Sundblom established the red, squat figure of Santa Claus as a basic western cultural image. Sundblom's father was originally Finnish, so Finland was at a very early stage linked to the commercial side of the story too. Nowadays Santas are generally dressed alike the world over in a red suit with white trim – there have even been attempts to create official or semi-official norms for his appearance – and Finland is no exception. There are even professionally organised courses for Santas which train them to visit private houses and serve market forces. A Santa that wears an awkward cardboard mask and the wrong colour of coat, who takes a glass or two to boost his confidence, is normally disapproved of, but no matter how amateur he is, he follows the old Finnish Christmas traditions more faithfully than his certified brothers.

Everyone agrees that the person who brings the Christmas presents must live in a mysterious place somewhere far in the North, but whether Santa Claus lives at the North Pole, in Canada, Norway, Sweden or Rovaniemi in Finland is a question that puzzles children writing their Christmas letters every year and keeps Nordic businessmen busy. Finns are of course sure that Santa's true home is in Korvatunturi and that the authentic tourist Christmas Land can only be located in Lapland, and this belief is becoming more widespread in other countries. The snow, the northern nature with its reindeers, and the midwinter darkness all create an excellent backdrop for the mystical figure that makes and delivers the presents, a figure that is at once strange and familiar and in whom the fears and hopes of childhood meet.

Juha Nirkko – Researcher, The Finnish Literature Society

88 SEURASAARI CHRISTMAS PATH

The idea for the children's Christmas path was born about 20 years ago, the product of two or three minds. We decided to bring it to life in a completely informal fashionby gathering a group of good people around us. All we needed were a total belief in what we were doing and the passion to carry it off.

We then began to market the event. First of all we sent messages to friends, neighbours and colleagues, and then to the Helsinki City authorities, the National Board of Antiquities, representatives of the church, NGOs and educational institutions. The idea to organize a non-commercial Christmas event for families with children was well received, and gradually it grew until we had plenty people and institutions participating.

The Christmas path is a one-day event, and it is held on the last Sunday before Christmas. We wanted the event to be outdoors in a beautiful location that would be reminiscent of bygone days. The only place that really fitted in Helsinki was the atmospheric Seurasaari Island. We hadn't a penny to our name but i the end we got Helsinki City to paya small sum for travel, materials and other necessities.

Had we agreed to advertise at the event we would probably have found sponsors quite easily, but we didn't want that. Luckily, however, we found some important partners that believed in our idea and did not lend their support on the basis of how much it might benefit their respective institutions. It was not money we wanted but equipment, expertise and voluntary labour. Thanks to these people we had e.g. transport, electricity, traffic attendants, splendid lighting and posters, and free Christmas porridge and gingerbread biscuits for the children. What amazing partners we found! Maija Karma the storybook illustrator painted a Christmas fairytale forest, and we spread this image on posters to playparks, daycare centres and after-school clubs.

The Christmas Path had a lot to offer visitors – there was singing and playing, storytelling, an activity course, a play, a labyrinth made of straw, and of course Santa Claus was there along with Mrs Claus too. We wanted to include children, so we asked them to bring a decoration that they had made themselves for the Christmas tree, and also a plate and spoon for their porridge. Children can easily participate in much of the programme. For adults, the most astonishing thing about it was that everything was free.

The Christmas path is now almost 20 years old. Us volunteers are in charge of the programme and Helsinki City is responsible for the infrastructure, such as different kinds of permits and the traffic among other things. New events have been added annually, including forest animals, elves, a peace candle park, and angel and gingerbread house exhibitions along with much more – there are about 30 different things along the path. They are easily coordinated because each separate feature has its own different person in charge. The patron of the event has been the president's spouse, who has come to greet the crowds along the path.

Organising outdoor events is always risky, but luckily the weather gods have been on our side. Last year's Christmas Path at Seurasaari attracted 10,000–20,000 visitors including many people from overseas, and there are now dozens of smaller Christmas Paths all over the country. It has certainly struck a chord!

The Christmas Path has also proved that daring, passion and co-operation can almost make miracles!

Marjaliisa Kauppinen – Creator of the Christmas path

89 FINNISH TANGO

Singer Reijo Taipale said that tango is the national anthem of Finland.

It took about fifty years for Finnish tango, meaning the Finnification of Argentinian tango in the 1940s and '50s, to be born. The evergreen "La Paloma" (1854), a fine example of habanera, the Cuban version of tango, became known in Finland in the 1890s, and Argentinian tango spread to Europe from Paris at the beginning of the 1910s. As far as is known, the first tangos were played in Finland in the summer of 1912 when a Romanian orchestra from St. Petersburg played Argentinian, Brazilian and Spanish tango-like songs at Kaivohuone restaurant in Helsinki. Other milestones were El Choclo (1905) and La Cumparsita (1917). The former was even recorded as a brass band arrangement while Finland was in the grip of tango fever in 1913. The first Finnish tango was composed in 1914 by Emil Kauppi as the accompaniment for a dance scene in a silent film.

Tango in the beginning was only one kind of dance among many others. Dance orchestras played Argentinian, German, Swedish and Lithuanian tangos in the 1920s and '30s, and there were also some Finnish ones, such as Matti Jäppilä's "Valkea Sisar", Juhani Pohjanmies's "Kuubalainen serenadi", Georg Malmsten's "Muistelo"and Valto Tynnilä's "Pienisydän". But real Finnish tangos only began to appear during the Second World War, with pioneering works from Arvo Koskimaa ("Syyspihlajan alla",1941) as well as Rober von Essen ("Kun ilta ehtii") and Helvi Mäkinen ("Kotkan ruusu") in 1942. Toivo Kärki started composing tangos a few years later while he was still serving as an artillery officer at the front, and he continued to release transcendent productions for several decades. His vocalists were the legendary Henry Theel and Olavi Virta, whose fantastically romantic and gypsylike glissando-rubato soon became the ideal for all tango singers. Pentti Viherluoto, Kaarlo Valkama, Unto Mononen and many others also composed tangos that later became evergreens.

The war itself cannot explain the emergence of Finnish tango, because themes like a fear of death, an uncertain future, home-sickness and war propaganda feature only occasionally in the music. More significant was that people gravi-tated towards their own familiar roots and the safe haven of national conservatism. New tangos no longer described the exotic "Argentinian pusta" but rather the desolate village roads. Literature research has demonstrated that the new tango lyrics reflected influences from both Finnish national poetry and Romantic literature: a person listening to the birds, left alone under a rowan tree or an old maple, or looking for a lily, a violet or another blue flower of longing. The "ardent melancholy" (Jukka Ammondt) of tango slyrics has often, especially abroad, been interpreted as a symbol of Finns' introversion and their feeling of inferiority and communication difficulties, but in reality it represents "silent information", a subtle way of handling painful matters. There are plenty of reasons for this: in the 1940s and '50s the new tango lyrics were written mainly by Kerttu Mustonen and other women who put their heart and soul into themes of love, agony and oblivion.

The musical aspect of Finnish tango also has its roots in distance places. The rhythm is the youngest, Argentinian ingredient of tango; it carries the tango's sexual message, an echo from the brothels of Buenos Aires and Montevideo that were visited by boastful coachmen and sailors. Finnish tango's rhythm is however somewhat more subdued: the macho syncopations of habanera and milonga have been diffused, the accompaniment has become more march-like, and the dance style has been transformed into a bashful walk. Nevertheless, the gender roles are still traditional: even in Finnish tango the man leads and the obedient woman follows. The firm bodily contact is a reminder of the presence of Eros, and its secret message can also be heard in the tango pulse: 140 beats per minute corresponds to the human heart rate in especially exciting situations. According to the Hite report, this heart rate is same as woman's when she experiences an orgasm!

In tango melodies one can hear both contrition and glimpses of heaven. The former is dominated by a descending quintet in a minor key. This is characteristic of ancient Finnish melodies, but its angst-releasing character originates from Gregorian and Protestant church music. The tangos of Unto Mononen (1930–1968) in particular are suffused with this musical influence, which has been adopted from passion chorals and cries for mercy. For example, "Satumaa", probably the most popular Finnish tango, instinctively reflects devotional cries for God's mercy.

"Satumaa" is a powerful image of Finnish agony, whereas the tangos composed by "the supreme god of Finnish popular song", Toivo Kärki (1915–1992), are much more tender in character. He was greatly influenced by East-European 19th century music, especially Russian romance, which was in fashion during the autonomous era. The ascending sixths in classic tangos like "Täysikuu", "Eron hetki on kaunis" and "Siks oon mä suruinen" bring light and consolation to the minor key and provide a modicum of heavenly joy with cut-glass chandeliers, champagne glasses and gypsy violinists. The Russian tradition has also been exploited by Pentti Viherluoto ("Punaiset lehdet" is probably the most Chekovian popular song ever composed), Lauri Jauhiainen and Reino Markkula, among others.

Finnish tango has given us hope and made our lives a little easier to live, and that is why it is like an unofficial national anthem.

Pekka Jalkanen – Composer

91 EVERYMAN'S RIGHT

Everyman's right is an ancient custom, based on tradition and to some extent national laws, which allows free access to land and waterways regardless of who owns the land. The sparse population of Finland and the other Nordic countries has provided a fertile soil for everyman's rights to develop from a system based on customary law to one encoded in the judicial system. This is in contrast to many other European countries, e.g. Belgium and England, where being on someone else's land is a criminal offence.

The most traditional everyman's right is probably the right to walk on other people's land. Walking, skiing or cycling across the countryside does not therefore require the landowner's permission.

The various everyman's rights have some features in common; no fees may be charged, and any incursion should be harmless and generally temporary, which means that roaming must cause as little disturbance as possible. Everyman's right to walk, ski or cycle does not apply to gardens or fields, which may not be traversed, and permission is always required for motor sledging. Organised e.g. skiing or orienteering competitions are not generally covered by everyman's rights, so an agreement with the landowner is necessary.

The particular regulations that apply to access to waterways are encoded in the Water Act. In principle any kind of vehicle may be used, and access is also permitted to frozen waterways. In certain areas there has been friction between people using jet-skis or noisy boats (e.g. for water skiing) and locals who live on the shore. This has been mainly caused by repetitive use too close to the land. In the ongoing reform of the Water Act it has been proposed that shoredwellers should be granted more protection by extending the penal code's provisions on domestic peace to apply to areas of water which are directly attached to a dweller's yard.

Temporary camping for one or two days is a well-known everyman's right, but lighting an open fire requires the landowner's permission. The camper is obliged to avoid creating any disturbance or nuisance and to observe the general prohibition on littering. Even the short-term parking of caravans requires the landowner's permission as a motor vehicle is involved.

Another typical everyman's right is the right to pick wild berries, mushrooms and flowers from anywhere that walking is permitted. More than half of Finnish households gather wild berries, and around 50 million kilos are picked annually. Some plants are however protected by the Nature Conservation Decree. Water may be drawn from waterways for household use and for e.g. animals, but taking soil from the bottom of waterways or elsewhere is prohibited.

Rod and baited hook fishing and ice-fishing are everyman's rights which are specifically prescribed in the fishing legislation. Approximately 40% of the population, i.e. 2 million people, participate in some kind of fishing event at least once a year.

Everyman's rights are generally accepted in Finland and have become established without comprehensive legislation. The rights attached to this ancient social innovation are not enjoyed by Finnish citizens alone, but also apply equally to anybody visiting our country.

Juha Korkeaoja – Minister of Agriculture and Forestry 2003–2007

91 EROTICISM IN EVERYDAY LIFE

The Finnish dictionary defines eroticism as follows: an aesthetic focused on sexual desire, especially the feelings of anticipation of sexual activity; not only the state of arousal and anticipation but also the attempt through whatever means of representation to incite those feelings.

I analyse these themes according to the year in which survey respondents were born and the year the survey was carried out. The year of birth reveals the historical period in which the respondent grew up, and by adding 10 or 20 years can we find out when the respondents learned the basics of sexual life. When the year that the survey was conducted is taken into account it is possible to analyse the sexual behaviour of people belonging to the same birth cohort as they age. The data was obtained from three Finnish sex-life surveys that were conducted in 1971, 1992 and 1999, and it is presented in several publications.

Several social changes which have occurred in the second half of the 20th century have had a direct affect on sexual life. The invention and development of contraceptive methods, especially the pill, has enabled people to have a more liberated sex life, while a lengthening human life span has influenced e.g. the way that adults live together, the number of sexual relationships they have, and gender equality within sexual relationships.

According to the surveys the majority of adult Finns are in steady sexual relationships, meaning that they are married or are otherwise committed, in common-law or steady relationships. The most common form of relationship is marriage: in 1971 two thirds of those aged between 18 and 54 were married, while in the 1990s it was one out of two. In the early 1970s only a few per cent of the population lived together out of wedlock but in the 1990s this was true of one in six. In 1971 every third young or middle-aged person was single, but there is no information on whether they had a steady partner. In the 1990s only one out of five people did not live with their sexual partner, but this figure does not include independent relationships, i.e. people who have a steady partner they do not live with. In the 1990s this type of relationship increased from 13% in 1992 to 15% in 1999. The amount of relationships has probably increased since the 1970s, although at the same time the proportion of married people has decreased.

Nowadays people have more premarital, consecutive and parallel relationships. While approximately 40% of women and 15% of men who were born at the beginning of the 20th century experienced sexual intercourse for the first time after getting engaged or married, the figure for those born at the end of the 1950s and later was approximately 5% for men and women alike. Parallel relationships have become more common among married people or people living together. This is especially true of women although men still have them considerably more often. The figures for parallel relationships and sexual partners were highest among men born between 1940 and 1960 and surveyed in the 1990s. Older people were still influenced by traditional sexual morals, while younger people had not yet had the opportunity to have relations outside their marriage etc.

Equality been the sexes is apparent with regards to sex. In the 1990s almost all Finns were of the opinion that women have as much right as men to initiate sexual interaction, but in the 1970s many women did not agree with this. In practice, the younger the woman the more likely it was that she participated alone or together with her partner in initiating the last time they had sex together.

Among the issues we looked at when we studied love and eroticism were; happiness in the relationship, ease in talking about sex, and mutual love. Happiness in relationships decreases with age; people born around 1950 were in 1971 considerably happier than they were in 1992 and especially 1999. Apart from age, the historical period influences the continuing happiness of the relationship. Young people born in 1970s, however, considered their relationships happier than their counterparts did in the 1950s.

The ease with which people can discuss their sex life with their partner seems to decrease with age. As with the happiness of the relationship, the historical period influences the perception of how openly and easily one can discuss sex with one's partner. The youngest respondents, who were born in the late 1970s, considered it easier to talk openly about their sex life with their partner than people born in the middle of the 20th century did when they were young.

Two thirds of all Finns between 18 and 54 years old felt that somebody loved them and somebody loved them back. Mutual love was more common in the 1990s than it was in 1971, and was spoken about by older men in particular who were surveyed in 1999. Older women had less chance of mutual love as men die earlier. In each survey the youngest were also without mutual love, but time is on their side.

Eroticism in everyday life has been transformed. The model of faithful monogamy has lost ground while gender equality with regards to sex has increased. Young peoples' relationships are nowadays happier and they find it easier to talk about their sex lives than their counterparts did before. The eroticism (happiness, conversation and mutual love) in a relationship decreases with age. Considering the whole population, not just people living in a relationship, it is clear that there is mutual love for older men but older women are frequently left without.

Elina Haavio-Mannila – Professor emerita in sociology, University of Helsinki

92 ICE-FISHING

The Ice Age retreated from Finland, leaving the Saimaa-Pielinen basin, approximately 9,500 years ago. Fishing has always been important, and even the first Fenno-Ugrian hunters who arrived in the area around 8,500 years ago understood its value. According to archaeological finds, hooks combining wood and bone were made by Fenno-Ugrian people at least as early as 4,000 years ago. Weights for angling that have been found in Stone Age settlements show that people already knew how to combine a sharp, angling part to a stone which functioned as a weight and a shaft.

Sharpened fishing spears have also been found in settlements dating back 5,000 years. The line has probably been made of e.g. nettles, animals' blood vessels or animal hair. The point of a Stone Age ice pick made of elk bone has also been found, so evidently the fishermen of the day were capable of breaking through the ice.

The history of ice-fishing goes back millennia, but without doubt the last decades have seen the number of ice-fishermen grow to unprecedented proportions, both in absolute and relative terms. According to tradition, modern ice-fishing was practiced in the 19th century by Cossacks, but they were hardly needed as instructors since ice-fishing for cod and perch has been professionally practiced for centuries. Herman Kaufman described his experiences on Hatanpää Bay in the city of Tampere in 1864–66 in his memoirs, describing how on winter mornings a number of the town's craftsmen and burghers gathered to ice-fish, or as he puts it "huddle on the ice practicing this most monotonous of amusements." They all sat perfectly immobile on ice sledges, and nobody seemed to get any fish. The ice sledge was quite essential, because at the end of the day the farmhands would arrive to pull the weakened burghers back to the town, and I assume that the farmhands were also needed to gouge the holes with an ice pick. Kaufman was mistaken however in his assessment of the future social importance of ice-fishing: "This healthy, fun and useful sport, which helped to while away the monotonous winter days, is probably gone for ever now. The times have changed and we change with them."

Ice-fishing has always had its adversaries, including the Grand Duchy of Finland, which suppressed winter fishing through the Fishing Act of 1902 which prohibited the use of a jig on the grounds that it damaged the fish. At that time people used fixed hooks, which foulhooked the body of the fish. The practice of angling spread to various parts of Finland before the Second World War, and was rapidly developed in the post-war period thanks to the skills that refugees from the Karelia region (innovation no. 66) brought with them, the clear division of labour and free time born of industrialisation, and the Fishing Act, which made fishing an everyman's right (innovation no. 91). The men who fought in the war enjoyed ice-fishing "thoroughly", fuelled as it was said to be by liberal amounts of alcohol. Pilkki, the Finnish word for ice-fishing, was adopted from Swedish in the 1950s. Most Finnish water areas are privately owned and administered by regional fishing authorities, and legislation decreed that a permit was required for ice-fishing, especially at the beginning of the 1950s. At that time the icefisher spent more time trying to catch permits than fish. The creation of fishing and ice-fishing associations (innovation no. 66) made it considerably easier to get permission however, and also served to defend the fishing rights of those who did not possess lands and water areas.

In Finnish society there is never any lack of persistence when it comes to fighting for a good cause. When a provincial fishing permission system was created in 1982, some felt that it would lead to a decline in perch stocks and the destruction of private jetties and saunas. Similarly, opponents of the 1996 Fishing Act predicted that it would have an adverse effect on private property and the Finnish Constitution. As a result, the Constitutional Law Committee (innovation no. 2) even had to assert in 1982 that "The fishing right that originates from the possession of a water area is a quite particular form of property". In fact, small-scale angling and ice-fishing allowed by everyman's rights or a provincial permit has not had a catastrophic effect on water area owners' fishing possibilities or the use of their other possessions, nor has it engendered the fragmentation of the Finnish society.

From the point of view of rural policy, recreational fishing and fishing tourism – including the ice-fishing competitions organised by families or work-mates – is a mine of unexploited possibilities.

Kari Rajamäki – Minister of the Interior 2004–2007

93 ICE SWIMMING

My mother once told me that, late one autumn, when I was only a couple of years old, I came into the house with my mittens soaked through. She asked me were my hands not freezing, and I answered that when I felt cold I warmed my hands in a muddy puddle.

I imagine that our ancestors have in the same empirical way noticed the warming effect that cold water has in certain conditions.

A few decades ago, having forgotten all about my childhood experience, I saw some people jumping into a hole in the ice in the crisp midwinter frost. Just watching made me shiver!

Then one December evening maybe twenty years ago I was in the old public sauna in Kruununhaka in Helsinki. A woman entered saying that she really wanted to go ice swimming, but the Christmas party she had attended the night before had taken its toll and she didn't feel up to it. We started talking about ice swimming and its effects. I said I had wanted to try it for a long time, but I didn't quite know where to go. She spoke highly of the winter swimming club she had joined (innovation no. 68) and told me what a nice place the small island behind the Hietaniemi cemetery was and how I could go there try it out. She also praised the place as a summer oasis and a good city substitute for a summer cottage.

So one August night the following summer I cycled to Ouritsaari Island. I opened the gate and stepped inside, where I was advised to climb the cottage stairs to the kitchen and ask for Liisa, who would tell me about membership. Liisa was at that time an 80-year-old winter swimming veteran who made fish soup and pancakes for the whole group in return for a nominal payment.

I was warmly received, and was immediately hooked by the club's cosy atmosphere. I had recently left my family and friends behind in Turku when I had moved to Helsinki to work after graduating, but suddenly with the winter swimmers I had a big reference group and a club where I always felt welcome, a part of the family. There was always someone to chat to if you felt like it, but you could also spend time on your own if you so desired.

The communalism of the winter swimming club worked in a way that I would like to see spread to modern Finnish society. At that time the sauna had a wood-burning stove which was tended by the club's senior members. The intergenerational relationships worked in a natural way, and everybody understood that those who worked could not just wander off in the middle of the day to heat the sauna. It was natural that those who were already free citizens looked after the heating, and they knew that the younger generations would follow on up the chain behind them.

The sauna as such is not a necessary element of winter swimming; it just makes it possible to dive in several times. Actually winter swimming with and without sauna is quite different. Swimming without a sauna rapidly produces a light and happy feeling, but on the other hand visiting the sauna between dives is significant in respect to the social aspect and as an aid to total relaxation.

My own experience of winter swimming is that it is the best sport around when it comes to social interaction, but it is difficult to explain to someone who has never practiced it how swimming in cold water can produce such a happy feeling. I say 'practiced' because mere experimentation does not, in my opinion, allow one to understand the feeling the winter swimmer gets once her body has learned to react to the cold temperature of the water – without exception experienced winter swimmers gasp elatedly as they rise from the icy hole. Swimmers generally chat and ask after those who have been absent. If nobody knows how they are then someone calls in or asks around. The oldest winter swimmers are currently over 90 years old.

In our club we wear swimming costumes, which makes it possible for men and women to mix. Many winter swimmers come with their spouses, and some even bring their families. In the sauna we exchange news, discuss the hot topics of the day and tell the latest jokes.

Winter swimming is a good way to unravel any knots that have formed during the day, and over the years I have drowned many sorrows, relieved a lot of stress, and been able to create space for new ideas. My life has acquired a new perspective.

Lately winter swimming has begun to grow rapidly and is becoming a popular sport. When I started swimming in Ouritsaari and asked what I needed, the answer was an old swimming costume, a towel and a pair of woollen socks, but the world has changed since then and we are being invaded with all kinds of modern shoes and gloves. The sport has become trendy, and many famous people who have started winter swimming give interviews on how often they swim and why. The one thing we have in common, however, is the good feeling we share.

Paula Kokkonen – Deputy Mayor of Helsinki 2004–2011

94 PESÄPALLO – FINLAND'S NATIONAL SPORT

Ball games were already being played in Finland in the 17th century, so the roots of pesäpallo, or pesis, the Finnish form of baseball, can be traced back centuries. Some ball games have the same roots as old mediaeval Scandinavian and German games. The popularity of ball games peaked in the late 19th century, when these amusing and playful pastimes united people in both cities and rural towns.

When Tahko Pihkala created pesis in 1922, he incorporated features from our old bat-andball games. Pesis, as a team sport, also represented the old tradition of communal activity. Some of Tahko's own inventions were the narrow field, which makes it more difficult to advance after each base, and the rule that the runner is out if a fielder catches the ball while the runner is not on a base. He also included aspects of American baseball. Pihkala created pesis specifically as the Finnish national sport – it was intended to encourage young people to play sport, unite the nation, and improve the capacity for national defence.

Although pesis is a national sport and cannot draw on the interest created by international competitions, it has remained steadily popular. One of the assets of pesis is that it suits all people of all ages and fitness levels, and it does not require expensive equipment or a special field to play. The game has always had a strong position in schools, and it is also a spectator sport, with top-level games being played across the country.

Pesis is currently played in Finland, Sweden, Switzerland, Great Britain, Norway, Australia, Germany, Estonia and New Zealand but, apart from Estonia, it is mainly played abroad by Finnish immigrants, who use it as a way of maintaining ties with their native country and national culture.

Pesis peaked in popularity during the postwar decades, a time of rapid industrialisation in Finland, but the nature of the game seems to make it best suited, not to an agrarian or industrial society, but to the current information society.

Pesis is also a competitive sport and its development has reflected the general development of competitive sports. However, it became too market-oriented during the latter part of the 1990s, which did this communal sport no favours at all. Profit seeking and rigged results almost destroyed the whole sport.

However, the pesis movement was able to see the crisis as an opportunity, and they decided that it should return to its origins and take the needs of contemporary society into account, so the idea of a Pesis Home Club Network of local pesis clubs was developed to provide communal activities for people of all ages. Through the Home Clubs, pesis can be seen not only as a competitive sport but also as an activity that helps to give meaning to life.

The Pesis Home Club Network plays a significant role in the cultural change affecting our society, and it has an impact on the evolving field of motion and sports and the development of civil activity. Through the Home Clubs, sports can promote both public health and learning.

Researcher Juha Hedman from the University of Turku has analysed the inclusion of sports in the public health model. He states: "Pesis enthusiasts have started the challenging process of founding Home Clubs. These are based on the Life as Learning programme, traditional national sports, and especially on the practice of passing knowledge down through the generations. In this context, individual learning occurs through responsibility (humbleness) and a strategic eye (self-confidence). The primary function of strategic learning with regards to both individuals and organisations is to find the optimal balance between these two basic characteristics."

Pesis is not only a versatile and imaginative sport – it is a social innovation which was born in an agrarian society as a result of Finnish creativity and a social need. And best of all, it can also be a social innovation in the developing information society.

The Pesis Home Club Network was held up as an example for reactivating citizens in the Citizen Participation Policy Programme report, which was submitted to the Minister of Culture at the time, Tanja Karpela, in 2006.

Markku Pullinen – Executive director, Pesäpallo union

95 NORDIC WALKING

Nordic walking in Finland has become a fashionable and established form of exercise. Approximately 800,000 people currently practice Nordic walking on a weekly basis and according to estimations more than 1.5 million Finns have at least tried it. Following the Finnish example, the boom has been somewhat explosive all over Central Europe and the other Nordic countries, and it is also spreading to other parts of the world.

It is hard to establish the beginning of Nordic walking – St Paul used a stick to keep wild animals away and Alpine people have always walked with the help of a staff. Although sticks have been involved in competitive sports in anaerobic hill exercises since the 1950s, it was at the end of the '80s that they really came into their own when the Central Association for Recreational Sports and Outdoor Activities (Suomen Latu) decided to organise a skiing trip to honour the statue of Tahko Pihkala, a Finnish athletics activist. There was no snow that day, however, so the trip had to be made by foot – but with the help of the skiing sticks. The father of the idea was Suomen Latu's executive director Tuomo Jantunen.

People became more and more interested in this kind of walking and, after the equipment had been sufficiently developed, the first Nordic walking poles came onto the market and the boom began. In 2001 I founded a Nordic walking group in the Finnish Parliament (innovation no. 1) which has attracted a very positive and constantly growing group of walkers. Every year, among other things, we elect the Parliament's Nordic Walker of the Year.

The health effects of Nordic walking have been studied and are overwhelmingly beneficial. In principle the activity suits anyone that can walk and observe their own body's exertion indicators. With the right height of pole and a good technique Nordic walking can be up to 40–50% more efficient than normal walking, and a prime additional benefit is that stress on the knees decreases by approximately 30%. Nordic walking suits people of all ages – from kids to grannies.

The general recommendation is to take a one-hour walk, during which one should be able to talk without losing one's breath. A regular one-hour walk twice a week maintains one's physical condition, while more regular walking will improve it.

Apart from making people physically fitter, Nordic walking also helps nurture a positive character, and is beneficial to mental health and weight control. Fat burning starts only after an hour of continuous walking, but it is also possible to lose weight.

Nordic walking has been tried out by all kinds of groups – in November 2000 the *Sotilasaikakauslehti* military magazine, which is published by the Finnish Officers' Union, organised a Nordic walking test in the Jaeger Guard Regiment, where conscripts in the Defence Forces Sports School participated in a 7 km walk wearing full combat gear. The exercise was completed 3 minutes faster with the walking poles than without them, and the perceived level of exertion was no higher. The time gained was mainly due to more efficient walking in the uphill stages. The conscripts considered the experiment a very positive experience.

It seems like Nordic walking is here to stay. There is great enthusiasm for it and it is only increasing – especially in the light of a survey from 1998 which found Nordic walking to be practically non-existent, while nowadays we are talking about millions of walkers throughout Europe. The Central Association for Recreational Sports and Outdoor Activities, Sport Institute of Finland and undoubtedly many other organisations as well as Nordic walking technique instructors and pole manufacturers have together created a versatile activity that makes it easier for people to keep in better shape.

Eero Akaan-Penttilä – Member of Parliament, President of the Parliament's Nordic Walking Club 1999–2011

96 DISH DRYING CABINET

The TTS Institute (Work Efficiency Institute) rationalised the Finnish kitchen in the 1940s. The starting point was challenging: in city apartments the kitchen and the servant's room were located in the darkest corner of the apartment, facing the yard, and the distance to the dining room was often long and complicated. In the countryside, cooking took place in the combined living room and kitchen in the midst of many other tasks, like living and sleeping. There was a lot of space, but no thought was given to the practicalities. Storage space was inadequate and scattered, and dishes were washed in metal washtubs.

Rationalisation was based on studies concerning the time used for household work and how strenuousness it was. About half of household work was related to food management. Standing, stretching, bending and carrying were strenuous and time consuming. Maiju Gebhard (the founder of the tts Home Economics Department in 1943) estimated that a woman's lifetime included 29,900 hours washing dishes, or 10 years of 8-hour working days, with no days off.

Rationalising the kitchen made it possible to reduce food management time by as much as three hours a day. Maiju Gebhard and Maija Kokko compared the working time in an old, unplanned kitchen with the time spent carrying out the same tasks in the same kitchen after it had been planned and equipped with efficient furnishings and utensils. The location of storage space had also been improved.

The first prerequisite for easing household work in the countryside was plumbing. A hot water supply was also important. As the dishwasher was a mere news topic from America at the time, Maiju Gebhard saw three ways of making dishwashing easier. The first was to make less dishes by using attractive cookware, in which the meal could also be served.

Another way was to arrange dishwashing as practically as possible by making space for dirty dishes, using good washtubs and hot water, and washing from right to left. The third way was to skip drying the dishes.

According to research done by the tts, drying the dishes on a good drying rack saved 0.5–2 hours working time daily. Towel laundry was reduced as well.

To keep the tops of the lower cabinets for other uses, the racks were fixed on the wall. To protect the dishes from dust, walls were added around the racks. The dish drying cabinet had come into being.

The first drying cabinet racks were made of wood, and it was the only piece of special kitchen furniture in many households.

The Home Economics Department of the tts developed models for kitchen furniture in the mid-1940s. American and Swedish studies as well as domestic experiments were used to formulate the dimensions. The tts sold technical drawings as well as cabinets produced in its own workshop.

Industrial production of kitchen cabinets started in 1948. Enso-Gutzeit's Tornator factory was the first to produce

Enso-cabinets based on the tts research. The cabinets had practical details such as wooden compartments for silverware and racks on the doors for saucepan lids.

The dish drying cabinet is still common in Finnish kitchens, even though dishwashers have become common now as well. It is now used for drying e.g. saucepans, freezer containers, vases and wooden and silver utensils. At the beginning of the 1990s the tts remodelled the dish drying cabinet, based on user research. The rack got a finer grid to keep small items from falling through, detergents and brushes got their own space, light plastic items such as baby feed bottles got a rack on the door, and a special basket for bottles was added. The lowest rack was for larger, heavier items, and the plate rack was located higher up.

Pirkko Kasanen – Ph.D., former research director,
TTS Institute

97 PUBLIC LAUNDERING JETTIES

"Washing carpets requires abundant water. The washing place must be such that while one part of the carpet is being brushed, its other parts are submerged in the water. After rinsing the carpet is not twisted but left to dry in a shady place on the grass or a rock." This was the advice on carpet washing that a Finnish household management course book supplied in 1938.

Abundant water and drying in the open air was possible only to those with their own shoreline, but urban people were able to wash their carpets properly too if they used municipal laundering jetties. Already in the 1890s there was a laundering jetty near the Hämeensilta Bridge in Tampere where carpets as well as other laundry could be washed, but over the years people began to do their laundry in common washhouses in the cities. Gradually households acquired washing machines to make life easier, but carpet washing places were still needed so laundering jetties became carpet washing jetties – and summer living rooms.

In Finland the traditional carpet is a rag rug, the composition of which is a triumph of ecological thinking and women's practicality. Rag rugs are made of rags that are carefully cut from old clothes and tightly bound together in a handloom. In spite of its name and raw material the rag rug has been an important textile in Finnish homes and a testament to the housewife's skill. A tight finish, straight edges and harmonic tones are the product of careful planning and weaving, so it was only natural that people wanted to keep them good and clean. Rag rugs are well suited to being washed on a jetty, and freshly washed carpets on the floor bring a lovely scent into the home.

Originally laundering jetties could be nothing more than two long boards on some big stones where women would squat down to work, but over time they became bigger and more solid constructions. Many consider the built-in barrels on the jetties, in which the washer could wash the carpets standing, as an important development because it saved a lot of backache. It was essential that the washing base was level because otherwise the carpet would wear down unevenly when it was scrubbed. From a waterlevel jetty it was easy to lift water and rinse the carpets.

Finns still wash their carpets on the shore, but municipal jetties have been relocated onto solid ground and linked to the sewer system, which decreases the burden on the clean water. An ecological washer washes her carpets clean without letting the dirty water run directly into the water system. There is no detergent that is totally harmless to nature, but it is the dirt that comes off the carpets that is the biggest environmental problem.

The carpet washer's equipment still includes water, a brush, pine soap and a picnic basket, but she cannot work at water level anymore. First the well-moistened carpet is brushed in the direction in which the rags lie on both sides, and for this a modern washer might use a long-handled brush or even a pressure washer to help. The traditional detergent is liquid pine soap, which is considered quite environment friendly and dissolves easily into the washing water.

Using plenty water to rinse is still the most important part of carpet washing. Inexperienced carpet washers can be recognised by carpets which have gone brown at the edges or in which the colours have bled into each other. Colours can be prevented from running by hanging the carpet in such a way that the water runs along the stripes. The brown colour is a sign of insufficient rinsing or too slow drying. Direct sunshine can fade the colours so it is necessary to dry carpets in the shade. Many washing jetties also feature a carpet mangle to squeeze out excess water before drying.

Carpet washing is still one of Finns' favourite outdoor summer activities. A good day for it is a sunny day with a warm breeze. The washers create a strong sense of community together, and reward themselves with treats from their hamper.

Pirkko Ruuskanen-Parrukoski – Excutive director,
The Finnish Federation of Settlements

98 DRY TOILETS

A toilet is almost as important as shelter, food and drinking water, but although it is a basic need, it is unfortunately not a human right. Almost a million people in Finland live outwith the municipal water supply and sanitation system. They are dry-toilet users.

In a vast, sparsely populated country it is not viable to lay pipelines everywhere, and dry toilets are anyway becoming more popular for environmental reasons. In Finland, people talk about toilets and the treatment of excrement as just another part of everyday life. Finland exports high-level education and expertise on water supply, sewerage and other related issues, and our knowledge of dry sanitation would be a fine complement on this, but it is not always taken into account.

On a global level the treatment of excrement – a basic need – remains a problem which lacks a sustainable solution. Only 5% of the world's population lives in an area with sanitation, and only around 50% of sewer systems lead to an appropriate water treatment station. One third of the world's population has never used a toilet.

The treatment of diarrhoea and other excrement-based infections ties up as much as half of the health care sector's scarce resources in developing countries. Using dirty water weakens people and kills children, the elderly and HIV-positive people. It is a serial killer which claims 5,000–6,000 children per day.

The Global Dry Toilet Club of Finland promotes the UN's Millennium Development Goals. The amount of people with no access to adequate sanitation could be reduced by half using economical and relatively simple methods. A properly implemented dry sanitation system prevents excrement-based pathogens from spreading. The waste is recycled as fertiliser, alleviating the hunger problem as phosphorus, a limited resource indispensable for growth, is returned to the nutrient cycle. Economically, socially and ecologically sustainable development reduces disease, hunger and poverty, and a common prerequisite for all of these is securing access to and protecting clean water. Sanitation is also a question of equality everyone should have safe access to a proper toilet, and no group of people should be forced to process other people's toilet waste while having no access to proper toilets themselves.

In 2006, the Global Dry Toilet Club of Finland organised the Second International Dry Toilet Conference, during which specialists from five continents met, updated, exchanged, analysed and shared information and experiences on sanitation and increased their expert knowledge. The content of the conference will be published as a book of abstracts and a Proceedings cd-rom. The conference was organised in concert with universities, since there is a shortage of education and appropriate course material in the field. Information on the field must be compiled, research developed, and practical solutions, installations and logistical processes tested. An exhibition which was organised as part of the DT 2006 Conference allowed manufacturers to access the accumulating information.

Asta Rajala – Former president, Global dry toilet club of Finland

99 MAD JOKES

Low self-esteem is one of mentally ill people's main problems, so in the 1990s the Finnish Central Association for Mental Health organised a diverse project to strengthen the low self-esteem of its members. One part of this was to collect jokes, anecdotes and stories about mentally ill people, mental hospitals and psychiatrists.

Association members were the main collectors, but mental hospital staff members were also invited to participate. The amount of material collected surpassed all expectations. The mentally ill people themselves were very enthusiastic, and in carrying out their task they learned to laugh at themselves, which is seen as a very important precondition for rehabilitation. About 90% of the jokes were gathered by people in rehabilitation.

There were around 850 jokes and anecdotes, of which the writer Kalevi Kalemaa used 400 to compile a book called Can you fish in the toilet bowl? The book received a lot of publicity and sold as many as 30,000 copies, which is quite a high number in the Finnish context. When the book was published, Kalemaa and the association's executive director Jussi Särkelä organised highly successful comedy events in different mental health associations across Finland.

Mary returned a toilet bowl brush she had bought two days ago to the shop.

- What's wrong with it? asked the salesperson.
- There might not be anything wrong with it at all, said Mary, but paper is much more convenient.

Although the feedback about collecting the jokes was mainly positive, there was also some resistance, e.g. from some mentally ill people who, understandably, were unable to accept jokes being made about such a serious issue. The most sensitive people, however, were mentally ill people's families, which can be explained by the fact that mental illness is a great burden on close relatives too. Another reason is that close relatives are often asked to carry more responsibility for the patient's welfare than they would have to if social services were better able to meet their needs with regards to care and rehabilitation.

The collecting of mental hospital jokes did not end with the book, but was spontaneously continued by some mentally ill people. One of the main hopes of the Finnish Central Association for Mental Health was realised in that the activity became decentralised and took place in local mental health associations. The improved self-esteem and empowerment of mentally ill people and the knowledge they gained about the important role that the association plays have had the effect of making the central association's strategies and policies more and more clearly influenced by the needs and wishes of grassroots members.

Jussi Särkelä – Non-fiction writer

100   STAR OF AFRICA

The first "Star of Africa" was printed in autumn 1951. A young Finn called Kari Mannerla had read about the world's biggest diamond, the Star of Africa and got hold of an English map of the continent. From it he randomly chose places that sounded exciting, and arbitrarily drew roads as well as shipping and flight routes, but it then occurred to him that players should be able to choose their own individual routes rather than follow a preset one. His most important idea however was the creation of tokens, which would be shuffled around and turned face down so that nobody would know what they would find in each place. More elements were added in the form of bandits and horseshoes.

Since his 14th birthday Kari Mannerla had designed dozens of other games with fanciful names such as Catch the Gangsters, Radium War on Mars, Horror of the Seas, Treasure of the Incas, etc, which he sold for small payment to the Koulutarpeiden keskusliike company. The old commercial counsellor used to see him coming and say, "Oh look, there comes the game boy again."

Star of Africa was the last game that Mannerla invented. He created it when he was 19 and sensed that it was pretty good. He offered it to the large publication house Tilgmann and, after a couple of years haggling over the price, finally settled for a rather humble cheque for a run of 10,000 games. He was however wise enough to set a condition that payment for any future runs would be negotiated separately, something that Tilgmann were happy to agree to since there were hardly ever any new editions of board games. But this time it was different. Another 10,000 were made the following year already, and one edition led to another. Over 100,000 Star of Africa games were sold in seven years.

After Tilgmann stopped marketing games in 1971 Star of Africa was made by Paletti and then since 1992 by its successor Peliko. Esko Eronen, the founder of Peliko, had already been responsible for Star of Africa while he was the director of Paletti, and has thus been associated with the game for more than 30 years now.

The millionth Star of Africa was sold in 1968, to a schoolgirl from Kuusamo, who was duly rewarded. 1.6 million Star of Africa games have now been sold in Finland, and almost 3.5 million worldwide. It is nearly as popular in Sweden, Norway and Denmark as it is in Finland, and has been played in e.g. Austria for more than twenty years. New markets are currently opening up in Russia, Estonia, Hungary and the Czech Republic.

Star of Africa never broke into the really big markets, probably because Mannerla did not start to promote it until the 1980s, which was too late. The world's leading game manufacturer in the United States was of the opinion that, as 1950s Africa was not currently fashionable, the game should be modified to take place in the Middle East, for example. To this Mannerla replied that in that case Tarzan should be moved to the Middle East as well. According to a German editor, Star of Africa was in no way different from other ordinary travel board games!

A big British publisher was enthusiastic but misunderstood the game and ruined it, which was unfortunate because the market for an English version would have covered half the world. Fantastic German, French and Italian versions were produced in Switzerland, but went off the market for some reason after only a couple of years.

When he retired Mannerla got into creating a card game version of the game, and more than 50,000 of these have been sold since 1996. In 1998 he signed a three-year deal with the Finnish Lottery Veikkaus for Star of Africa scratch cards, of which more than 10 million have been sold. In 2006 Mannerla created "Treasure of the Incas", a modified version of Star of Africa set in South America, which, like the original, was an overnight success. A computer game version was also created by the Finnish Amer Corporation, but it was launched at a bad time and did not succeed.

Mannerla spent his working life in the advertising business. He started as a 17-year-old trainee in Ad Agency sek and retired after 55 years from his post as president of the board.

Kari Mannerla – Inventor of the Star of Africa